# THE SATIRE OF
# JONATHAN SWIFT

*This book contains three lectures delivered at Smith College in May, 1946, and constitutes the first of a projected series of volumes of Smith College lectures.*

# The Satire of

# JONATHAN SWIFT

*by*

HERBERT DAVIS

THE MACMILLAN COMPANY

NEW YORK, 1947

Copyright, 1947, by
THE MACMILLAN COMPANY

First Printing

*In memory of*

WILLIAM ALLAN NEILSON

# CONTENTS

# THE SATIRE OF
# JONATHAN SWIFT

# INTRODUCTION

*Satyr is a sort of Glass, wherein Beholders do generally discover every body's face but their Own; which is the chief Reason for that kind of Reception it meets in the World, and that is why few are offended with it.*

WHETHER or not that is the reason for the reader's satisfaction there can be no doubt that it is for his satire that Jonathan Swift is read, and will continue to be read. And this explanation of the effect of satire does account for the fact that people of all parties can equally enjoy and even applaud the strokes of a satirist like Swift. Two hundred years after his death he is remembered not perfunctorily, not just by scholars or collectors, but by those who would use his satire for their own present purposes. In London and Dublin the echoes of his voice might be expected to reverberate from Marlborough's wars to Churchill's wars, from Dublin's struggle against dependency on the Whig government of George I to Dublin's present independent neutrality. But his satire is no less alive and satisfying to the reader in an America staggering beneath the weight of her

1

destructive powers, and it is being equally acclaimed and widely disseminated in the Soviet Union where for the first time a Russian translation of *A Tale of a Tub* has been allowed to appear, and where *Gulliver's Travels* has been recently translated into twenty-eight different languages for the Soviet peoples.

I do not, therefore, feel it necessary to apologize for venturing to choose at this time for the subject of these lectures the satirical writings of one who was very decidedly a Tory and a Churchman, though often an embarrassment both to the Church and to the Tories, being (as a contemporary called him) "one of the greatest *Droles* that ever appear'd upon the Stage of the world"; and who was also an Irishman, not merely in the sense that he was born and died there and was Dean of St. Patrick's, Dublin, but so deeply concerned with the Irish cause that he earned the name of Hibernian Patriot, and further, like many another Irishman, provided very good arguments for the Americans in their struggle for independence. He remains none the less, and would wish to be regarded, an English gentleman, a close associate of men like Sir William Temple, Lord Somers, Oxford and Bolingbroke, and the friend of Pope, Arbuthnot and Gay. Most of his books were published in London, and those that appeared first in Dublin, including a great many that were mistakenly attributed to him there, were quickly picked up by the London booksellers and reprinted for a market in which he was a certain best-seller.

In the last two hundred years, moreover, since Swift's death, his works have been repeatedly re-edited, and he has been the subject of Remarks, Observations, Lives, Studies, and lectures which have shown the different fashions of the time only in their varying attitudes; he has been admired and disliked with equal intensity, but never ignored. And during the revival of interest in eighteenth-century studies which has taken place in the last forty years, a great deal of useful work has been done to establish more carefully the canon of his writings, to provide for the first time a reliable edition of his *Poems,* a well-arranged and fully annotated edition of his *Correspondence,* together with new editions and studies of the *Prose Works* necessitated by the considerable amount of new manuscript material and bibliographical information which has recently come to light.

I speak of these editions, of this textual and bibliographical work, not, I hope out of any foolish sense of the importance of my trade as an editor, but to emphasize that there is no excuse for us to neglect the close study of Swift's own writings to follow the lure of such intriguing problems as his personal relationships with Stella and Vanessa, or to try and find some scientific explanation for the violence of his dislike for certain qualities of the human species, or to theorize about some dark secret of demoniacal possession or Freudian complex according to the prevailing fashion of the day.

I shall speak, therefore, only of the main satirical writings of Swift in which he continues to live most powerfully. I shall examine his work at three different levels which happen to fall into three separate periods of his life, according to a very simple pattern which almost inevitably shapes the work of every writer and artist. The first shows him in his relation to his art and may be called aesthetic; the second, in his relation to society and may be called political; the third, in his relation to moral and permanent values and may be called ethical. These parts or divisions of a writer's work are in fact never entirely separate or found in a regular sequence. Nevertheless, I believe it is not very dangerous and might not be unprofitable to risk such a simplification. For every craftsman must begin by an apprenticeship to his own particular trade; he must first learn to handle his tools and to know his materials. He will be interested in the work that the successful masters are doing; he will tend to pick up the particular language of the trade, the shop-talk. His world will be the world of his art and of his fellowcraftsmen. He may extend that further by becoming interested in the craftsmanship of earlier generations or in new technical devices, or in the common problems of those working in other allied arts; or he may be interested in theoretical or practical criticism. He will be practising his art and developing his technical skill and his knowledge, enjoying the free play of mind and imagination in a world of its own, detached, a world of what may be called aesthetic values.

There are some (artists and prophets), who remain so preoccupied with the problems of their art or with their own visions that they continue to live apart and refuse to allow themselves to be involved in the social struggles or the political factions of their own times. "Let no one marvel," says Vasari, "that Michelangelo loved solitude, for he was devoted to art which claims men for itself alone; and because those who study must avoid society, the minds of those who study art are constantly preoccupied, and those who consider this to be eccentricity are wrong, for he who would do well must avoid cares and vexations, since genius demands thought, solitude and comfort, and a steadfast mind." It must not be forgotten that many of those who have avoided or spurned the burden of public office and refused to be wearied by temporal power have not always been self-indulgent escapists, but have often been stirring witnesses against the follies of their times and against man's inhumanity to man; they have left in their art a permanent memorial, a negative criticism as it were, of the political and social questions of their day. There are others, however (historians and philosophers as well as scholars and artists), who have been equally men of action, playing a central part in the public life of their time, or at least much in society, whose creative work has seemed to be but the flowering of a life of action. In public office or in the service of a cause they have used their gift as orators or writers for an immediate purpose. Their speeches and pamphlets have been acts intended to bring about certain events, to rouse their people to war or to change a mode of government. Such writings have their origin in the circumstances of the time. They may even have little to do with the expression of the individual genius of the artist; his spirit is subdued and bent to a purpose beyond his control, outside forces lend him their power. This kind of writing can only be done by one who actually has the responsibility of action, and by one who is living at the center of affairs. This kind of art does not depend on comfort and could not proceed out of quiet and solitude.

This was the situation of Swift at the height of his political influence in London during the last

years of Queen Anne's reign. In a letter addressed
to him at that time Archbishop King reminded him
that "a man's spirit is never more awakened nor
his thoughts better, than in the intervals of a hurry
of business" and encouraged him to continue to
write on subjects suitable to his calling; quoting as
examples Caesar, "who wrote amid the hurry and
fatigues of a general," and Erasmus, "whose life
was almost a continual journey." At that very time
Swift was, like Caesar, writing his commentaries
and in the midst of his press of business keeping an
intimate journal of his activities; but he was also
using to the utmost his satirical powers as well as
his facility in popular verse, in performance of his
official duties as, in modern terms, director of
publicity for the Tory ministry.

He is writing no longer as a wit, a young gentleman much in the world, showing off his skill as he
makes fun of the world of religion and learning; he
is now using his pen to get certain things done. His
work is affected by qualities of expediency. He must
calculate its effect upon a particular audience at a
particular moment; and as long as he is thus concerned with a party and a cause, and engaged in the
performance of his official duties, there will inevitably be limits to the scope of his work, however
fully it may draw out all his powers. He will need
to use some of his weapons with great care; some-

7

times he may have to ignore the subtleties of a situation and simplify his arguments almost to crudity to get the required effect. However enlightened he will have to take the risk of seeing his human sympathies narrowed, his values tarnished by being absorbed in a party campaign or in a national or popular cause. But if, like Milton or like Swift, he is fortunate enough later to be removed from the service of temporal power and left in retirement and isolation to observe and remember and set down a record for posterity, he may be freed again for a final creative effort, in which all the qualities of his genius will be given free play whether they appear clothed in the grandeur and dignity of an epic or masquerading in a volume of lying Travels.

It is only in this final stage that the writer wins complete freedom. He is established as a master of his craft and is unaffected by, or able to use as he wills, the fashions of the literary world in which he has gained his reputation; and he is completely master of his material, untroubled by any concern with the immediate effect on a party or a cause, writing for posterity and dealing with moral values and human qualities with a power which enables him to break through the boundaries of his own time and place and leave his work among the permanent memorials of the human spirit.

# I

## LITERARY SATIRE

'Tis own'd he was a Man of Wit—,
Yet many a *foolish thing* he writ—;
And, sure he must be *deeply* learn'd—!
That's more than ever I discern'd—;
I know his *nearest friends* complain
He was too *airy* for a Dean—.

BEFORE the publication of *A Tale of a Tub* in 1704, Swift had appeared in his own person in the world of letters only as an editor of the *Letters of Sir William Temple*. The first two volumes were printed in 1700 with a dedication in which he humbly presents them to his Most Sacred Majesty William III, describing himself as a domestic chaplain to his Excellency the Earl of Berkeley, one of the Lords Justices of Ireland. A third volume was printed in 1703. But he evidently felt that in his role as a satirist, he would be hampered and restricted if he were to appear in this way, wearing a parson's gown and associated with such respectable connections. There had been, indeed, in the seventeenth century, a splendid tradition among the most reverend and eminent divines in their controversial treatises about serious matters which would seem to sanction, as Anthony Collins pointed out in his *Discourse concerning Ridicule,* the use of "Insult, Buffoonery, Banter, Ridicule, Irony, Mockery and bitter Railing"; and after the Restoration

11

this tendency was further encouraged by a Court
audience led by "a King who had a disposition to
banter and ridicule everybody" and "some of the
greatest Droles and Wits that any Age ever pro-
duc'd." But tastes were changing at the end of the
century, and Swift himself was then under the influence of Sir William Temple, who had solemnly
and vigorously denounced the taste for satire, and
had probably prevented Swift from publishing *The
Battle of the Books* in 1698.

At any rate we know that Swift put aside this and
other satirical papers of his own which he had been
working at in 1696-7, and took precautions that
when they did appear he would not necessarily be
involved, until he could see what sort of reception
they would have. He felt that he needed for his purpose the fullest freedom to range at will over the
whole field of letters, for he wished to make sport
with all the foibles of the Grub-street brotherhood
as well as the societies of Gresham and of Wills, the
hack-writers and fashionable poets, the virtuosos
and the wits, and "to expose the numerous corruptions in religion and learning, which might furnish
matter for a satire that would be useful and diverting." He chose therefore to appear as an unknown
young gentleman of taste and learning dedicated to
the high task of serving the Church and the State by
diverting the attacks of the wits who occupy them-

selves in picking holes in the weak sides of religion and government; and in such a task—which he claimed should win him the approval of all good men—he would be justified in letting loose all his powers to expose the shams of the time and to make merry at the expense of all hypocrites and dullards. But his attack must be made in "a manner altogether new, the world having been already too long nauseated with endless repetitions upon every subject."

The author of *A Tale of a Tub* is presented to us as at the maturity of his powers—"his invention at the height, and his reading fresh in his head, a young gentleman much in the world, who wrote to the taste of those who were like himself." He is not without a certain youthful insolence, contemptuous alike of stupidity, dullness and pedantry, addressing himself to those who have enough wit to appreciate irony, and enough knowledge to recognize parody. He has had sufficient experience to know that he need not be afraid of those who will be provoked to anger and fury by his satire. They deserve only his scorn:

There is a Brain that will endure but one Scumming: Let the Owner gather it with Discretion, and manage his little Stock with Husbandry; but of all things, let him beware of bringing it under the Lash of his Betters; because, That will make it all bubble up into Impertinence, and he will find no

13

new Supply: Wit, without Knowledge, being a Sort of Cream, which gathers in a Night to the Top, and by a skilful Hand, may be soon whipt into Froth; but once scumm'd away, what appears underneath will be fit for nothing, but to be thrown to the Hogs.

This is still in the manner of the seventeenth century, in the true line of wit; the vivid image of the whipped cream, possibly picked up from his reading of François de Callières, who had used it simply as a symbol for writing "large in appearance but little in substance," but here elaborated and played with and worked to the utmost, until the froth vanishes and we are left with another even more powerful image of the skimmed milk fit only for the hogs. A careful contemporary reader would have recognized the method, and might have been reminded of another fantastic image of scorn in a popular satire of the preceding generation, which the author of *A Tale of a Tub* admired and referred to, *The Rehearsal Transpros'd* by Andrew Marvell. He also is describing the brain of his adversary:

You have, contrary to all architecture and good economy, made a snow-house in your upper roome, which indeed was philosophically done of you, seeing you bear your head so high as if it were in or above the middle region, and so you thought it secure from melting. But you did not at the same time consider that your brain is so hot, that the wit

14

is dissolv'd by it, and is always dripping away at the icicles of your nose. But it freezes again, I confess, as soon as it falls down; and hence it proceeds that there is no passage in my Book, deep or shallow, but with a chill and key-cold conceit you can ice it in a moment, and slide shere over it without scatches.

There is the same playful extravagance and exuberant gaiety in these conceits, but Swift's sentences show an economy and strength, and a power of invention—to use the phrase of the time—which seems to me to justify his claim that his wit was all his own. He speaks of having read Marvell with pleasure, and evidently took good heed of his warnings addressed to those who would take upon themselves the envious and dangerous employment of being writers.

For indeed, whosoever he be that comes in print, whereas he might have sate at home in quiet, does either make a treat, or send a challenge to all readers; in which cases, the first, it concerns him to have no scarcity of provisions, and in the other, to be compleatly arm'd; for, if anything be amiss on either part, men are subject to scorn the weakness of the attaque, or laugh at the meanness of the entertainment.

There is no scarcity of entertainment in the fare Swift provides, no lack of weapons for the attack. The manner of his attack may seem at first sight

15

very conventional, for it was a favourite conceit of the time to refer to the custom of seamen to throw out a tub when they meet a whale to divert it from attacking the ship. It must have been well known to all Swift's readers, as it occurs in such popular books as this satire of Marvell's I have been referring to, and in the prefatory Remarks to the Reader in Francis Osborn's *Works*, which had reached a seventh edition in 1673:

> I only threw it out like an empty cask to amuse him, knowing that I had a whale to deal with, . . .

and again:

> . . . in immitation of Sea-men, I may perhaps by design have cast out some empty stuff, to find play for the Whale-mouthed gapers after Levity; lest they should spoil the Voyage.

Swift's parable is very obvious, where the whale symbolizes Hobbes's *Leviathan* and the ship in danger the Commonwealth, though again he does not miss the opportunity to enlarge the conceit, rather confusing the picture, as the waters round the Leviathan positively seethe with tubs, namely "Schemes of religion and government, whereof a great many are hollow, and dry, and empty, and noisy, and wooden, and given to rotation." He will himself provide for the purpose *A Tale of a Tub*. Again neither the phrase nor its use as a title is new. Instances are

16

given in the Guthkelch and Nichol Smith edition,
to which I am indebted throughout, of its common
use in the sixteenth and seventeenth centuries, in the
sense of "an idle discourse," or as explained in the
title of a lost work "a gallamaufrey of merriment."
Swift hooks the two ideas together and has a title
for a gallimaufry of merriment in which he can
make fun of everything that catches his fancy not
only as he looks around him in the world of contemporary controversy, but as he looks back across
the troubled waters of the Revolution and the Commonwealth and the Civil War to the serene shores
of that age immediately before the troubles which
he always regarded with longing and pride as the
time of England's highest glory both in life and
in letters.

For the real object of Swift's satire in the *Tale* is
the corruption he saw in English letters during the
latter half of the seventeenth century, destroying
what he felt had been its finest achievements. This
belief is repeatedly stated, and never modified. He
first stated it in the *Tatler*, dated September 28,
1710, satirizing current affectations of language, and
clearly setting forth what he regarded as the stand-
ards of good taste in English, namely that simplicity
which is unaffected by modish fashions, "such as the
writings of Hooker, a country clergyman, and of
Parsons the Jesuit, both in the reign of Queen Eliz-

abeth . . . much more clear and intelligible than those of Sir H. Wotton, Sir Robert Naunton, Osborn, Daniel the Historian, and several others who writ later; but being men of the Court, and affecting the phrases then in Fashion; they are often either not to be understood, or appear perfectly ridiculous."

He stated it very plainly in his *Letter to the Lord Treasurer,* emphasizing the corruptions in language "from the Civil War to this present time"; first, the enthusiastic jargon prevailing during the usurpation, and then the licentiousness which entered with the Restoration, which from infecting religion and morals fell to corrupt the language, as shown in the plays and other compositions written for entertainment during the next fifty years. He stated it again in *A Letter to a young Clergyman,* written in Ireland ten years later, and again in a slightly different form in the *Essay on Conversation,* as, for example:

> I take the highest period of politeness in England (and it is of the same date in France) to have been the peaceable part of King Charles I's reign.

It is obvious from this on which side Swift would find himself in the controversy between the Ancients and the Moderns which had been sharpened by the recent claims for precedence made on behalf of the latest discoveries and developments in the world of science and letters. He was indeed inclined to be unduly sceptical of the importance and value of the new sciences and more aware of the corruptions than of the improvements in modern learning. He was not therefore led into the fray entirely to defend Sir William Temple against the attacks made on his *Essay upon the Ancient and Modern Learning,* although this episode provided him with an excuse to join with the Christ Church wits against Bentley and Wotton. At the same time it forced him to uphold a very weak case, as Temple had stated it in his Essay, and he was obliged to rely on the effectiveness of the literary devices he used to get the better of his opponents. The main device is indicated by the title—A Full and True Account of the Battle Fought last Friday, Between the Antient and the Modern Books in St. James's Library. This looked like an imitation of François de Callières's *Histoire poétique de la Guerre nouvellement déclarée entre les Anciens et les Modernes* though Swift afterwards said he had never heard of it. But there were many advantages in handling the subject in a mock heroic fashion as a battle between the actual volumes in the King's Library, which Bentley had confessed was in a state of dirt and confusion. The Homeric conflict takes place "on the plains of St. James's Library"—a phrase which is just enough to carry us into a mock heroic world remote from the actual controversy and the arguments over the genuineness of the Epistles of Phalaris. In this world Swift can

19

play with the reader as he will; it is only a matter of opposing Dryden to Virgil, and describing his steed and his arms in Hudibrastian fashion:

Behold, upon a sorrel Gelding of a monstrous Size, appear'd a Foe, issuing from among the thickest of the Enemy's Squadrons; But his speed was less than his Noise; for his Horse, old and lean, spent the Dregs of his Strength in a high Trot, which though it made slow Advances, yet caused a loud Clashing of his Armor, terrible to hear.

. . . the Helmet was nine Times too large for the Head, which appeared Situate far in the hinder Part, even like the Lady in a Lobster, or like a Mouse under a Canopy of State or like a shrivled Beau from within the Penthouse of a modern Periwig.

In similar fashion he describes Bentley and Wotton "like two Mungrel curs prowling around" who steal the armour of Phalaris and Aesop while they are asleep; and the final exploit of Boyle who appears like a young lion, and hunts the two of them until finally his lance pierces them together:

As, when a skilful Cook has truss'd a Brace of Woodcocks, He, with Iron Skewer, pierces the tender Sides of both, their Legs and Wings close pinion'd to their Ribs; So was this Pair of Friends transfix'd, till down they fell, joyn'd in their Lives, Join'd in their Deaths.

If this were all, however, we should feel that Swift had done no more than provide a trivial diversion to draw attention away from the real conflict. But again in the midst of the allegory, as in the *Tale*, he introduces a digression: and a very fitting one, as the dispute was also concerned with Aesop, who was praised by Temple as the most ancient of the ancients and was recognized by all ages as the greatest master in this kind. Very fitly also in the dirt of St. James's Library, Swift discovers a large spider's web, in which a bee, entering through a broken pane of the window, has become entangled. This occasions a dispute between them which is then interpreted by Aesop, who had listened to them "with a world of pleasure."

The fable and the interpretation of it are Swift's real contribution to the debate between the Ancients and the Moderns; and it is not surprising that a hundred and fifty years later, when the debate had taken another form, Swift's phrase "sweetness and light" was carried as a banner by a young apostle of culture as he advanced against the hosts of the Philistines. It was also a triumphant vindication of the art of Aesop, no matter what Bentley had done to his title page and half of his leaves. The fable is made out of a proverb, evidently common, as it is frequently turned to literary use in the seventeenth century: "Where the bee sucks honey, the spider sucks poison." Here we can observe it expanding into a lovely form, as it is dramatized in Bentley's

21

library, and elaborated with mock heroic language, and finally interpreted as a symbol of the dispute between the Ancients and the Moderns:

> For, pray Gentlemen, was ever any thing so Modern as the Spider in his Air, his Turns, and his Paradoxes? He argues in the Behalf of You his Brethren, and Himself, with many Boastings of his native Stock, and great Genius; that he Spins and Spits wholly from himself, and scorns to own any Obligation or Assistance from without. Then he displays to you his great Skill in Architecture, and Improvement in the Mathematicks . . . yet, if the materials be nothing but Dirt, spun out of your own Entrails (the Guts of Modern Brains) the Edifice will conclude at last in a Cobweb: The Duration of which, like that of other Spiders Webs, may be imputed to their being forgotten, or neglected, or hid in a Corner. . . . As for Us, the Antients, We are content with the Bee, to pretend to Nothing of our own, beyond our Wings and our Voice: that is to say, our Flights and our Language; For the rest, whatever we have got, has been by infinite Labor, and search, and ranging thro' every Corner of Nature: The Difference is, that instead of Dirt and Poison, we have rather chose to fill our Hives with Honey and Wax, thus furnishing Mankind with the two Noblest of Things, which are Sweetness and Light.

It was a nice compliment to Temple to use the bee as the symbol of the Ancients; for some of Swift's readers would remember Temple's *Essay on Poetry,*

where he compares the poet's art with the activities
of the bees in a passage which Swift in that last sentence condensed with great precision:

> Bees must range through Fields as well as Gardens,
> chuse such Flowers as they please and by Proprie-
> ties and Scents they only know and distinguish:
> They must work up their cells with admirable Art,
> extract their Honey with infinite Labour, and sever
> it from the Wax, with such Distinction and Choice,
> as belongs to none but themselves to perform or to
> judge.

Some of Swift's readers would also remember this
passage, to which Professor F. P. Wilson drew my
attention, in Bacon's *Novum Organum:*

> The men of experiment are like the ant; they only
> collect and use; the reasoners resemble spiders,
> who make cobwebs out of their own substance.
> But the bee takes a middle course, it gathers its
> material from the flowers of the garden and of the
> field, but transforms and digests it by a power of
> its own. Not unlike this is the true business of
> philosophy.

In the *Battle of the Books* Swift shows what side
he is on, and he succeeds by his wit and humour,
and by the power of his style. But he does not reveal
there as he does in the *Tale* the extent of the prepa-
ration he had undertaken so that in offering entertainment to his readers, he should not be criticized
for any scarcity of provisions. As an undergraduate

at Trinity College he had had no great reputation
as a scholar; but we happen to have some interest-
ing information about his reading during those years
when he was planning and working on the *Tale*. I
commend to you the account of his reading in Professor Nichol Smith's Introduction:

> During the third and most important period of
> his residence (at Moor Park), from May 1696 till
> Temple's death in January 1699, he employed his
> leisured independence in varied and constant
> study. The *Tale* was written mainly, if not wholly,
> at this time. He wrote it from a full mind.

The list of his reading which we have for the whole
year 1697 indicates the breadth and variety of his
reading, including, in addition to French and English authors, the Iliad and the Odyssey, Virgil twice,
Lucretius three times, Horace, Cicero's Epistles, Pe-
tronius, Lucius Florus three times, Diodorus Sicu-
lus, Cyprian, Irenaeus and Sleidan's commentaries.
"This—says Professor Nichol Smith—gives only a
fraction of the reading that went to the making of
the *Tale*," but "it admits us, as it were, to a secret
view of Swift's habits of mind when he was gaining
his full powers, and Swift never wrote anything that
gives a greater sense of sheer power than some of
the later sections of the *Tale*."

It is unlike the rest of his writings, because it is
so literary, so full of echoes from his reading, and so

concerned with the world of letters, the world that at that time he knew best, because he had been living entirely in it. For he had been exercising himself in the art of writing as well as filling his mind. The *Tale* represents only a very small portion of all that he had written during the last ten years of the century. I do not refer to his own simple statement that "in the author's original copy there were not so many Chasms as appear in the Book," I am thinking rather of his early experiments in poetry, and the impression left from those that survived, those Pindarics in which he seems to have wished to compete with Cowley and the experiments in heroic verse, not much less restrained in manner. He soon discovered that such forms would not fit the kind of thing he wanted to say, and contemptuously turned away from these poetic exercises, not even including them in any of his later collections of verse. Nevertheless there is to be observed in them a force and energy, struggling with the too voluminous folds of flowing rhetoric and showing the ferment of thought in which he lived. In his attack on the extravagancies of the previous age, he benefited by these struggles in which he had won his freedom as perhaps every young writer has to do from the prevailing forces round about him, in order to shape his art to fit his own individual purpose. These Odes, addressed to the King, to Sir William Temple, to Archbishop Sancroft, and the Epistle to Mr. Congreve begin in a dignified strain of compliment, and were evidently intended to serve the same purpose as those later presented by Congreve on suitable occasions as an offering to the King on his taking of Namur, or lamenting the Death of our late Gracious Queen Mary of ever blessed Memory. But unlike the cool marbled smoothness of Congreve's lines, Swift's gather a tempestuous motion and quickly become roughened by moods of anger and satire, giving vent to his hate,

> whose lash just heaven has long decreed
> Shall on a day make sin and folly bleed;

and he breaks off apologizing for his unfitting outbursts:

> Perish the Muse's hour, thus vainly spent
> In satire, to my Congreve's praises meant;
> In how ill season her resentments rule,
> What's that to her if mankind be a fool?

And in the last of these poems addressed to Temple in December 1693, he renounces the Muse as a delusion and a deceit,

> Troubling the Crystal fountain of the sight,
> Which darts on poets eyes a trembling light;
> Kindled while reason sleeps, but quickly flies
> Like antic shapes in dreams, from waking eyes:

The experience which gives such force to some of the lines of this poem, in which he turns away forever from the fond delusions of a youthful poet's romantic dreams, is the source of the irony and gives a sort of personal colouring to the triumphant scepticism of the Digression on Madness in the *Tale*, where human happiness is defined as "a perpetual possession of being well deceived," and the same struggle between fancy and reason is examined:

> But when a Man's Fancy gets astride on his Reason, when Imagination is at Cuffs with the Senses, the common Understanding, as well as common Sense, is kick't out of Doors; the first Proselyte he makes, is himself.

I have tried to indicate briefly how well prepared Swift was in 1697, as a young man of thirty, for the role of the Author of *A Tale of a Tub*, not only by his hard reading and study and contemplation, but also by the vigorous exercise of his imagination and his skill in the various forms of his art. Now I should like to examine the *Tale* itself to try and show the devices he used to gather into it so much of the spirit of the century that was nearing its close, its enthusiasm, its pedantry, its shams, its conceits, and all the richness and extravagance and variety of its strange faiths and hopes and delusions. For the paradox is—and it would miss its purpose if it were not paradoxical—that the work is a product of the seventeenth century, entirely characteristic in form and manner, and at the same time a repudiation and

criticism of all the most vigorous literary fashions of
the previous sixty years.

For example in its outward shape and form it ob-
viously resembles the work of those writers whom
Swift repudiates, rather than the work of those like
Hooker and Parsons, whose style he admired. And
it is equally unlike himself, as Dr. Johnson pointed
out, going so far as to question indeed whether Swift
could have written it: "It has so much more thinking, more knowledge, more power, more colour, than
any of the works which are indubitably his." This
impression that the *Tale* is unlike Swift in having
more colour, more evidence of his reading and
knowledge of literature, is due to the fact that he
has put into it so much material from the world of
letters in order to make play with it and to shake
himself free from it. It is also due to the element of
parody in its whole design, a feature indeed constant in Swift's satire and he would say inevitably
so, because he believed that it would be impossible
for any satirist to imagine or create affectations
which could serve his purpose as well as those plen-
tifully to be found in life or literature. And parody
to be perfect should be as close to the original as
possible. Therefore since certain affectations in the
world of letters usually appeared in certain particular places, e.g. in *Dedications,* or *Digressions,* or
*Prefaces,* or *To The Readers,* what could be more

28

fitting than to fit out the *Tale* with all these append-ages, so that the proper place would be available to exhibit and expose such follies? In order to make sure that his method would not be misunderstood by later readers, Swift was careful in the *Apology,* which he added as a further preface in 1710, to ex-plain exactly what he was doing and who were his victims.

There is one Thing which the judicious Reader cannot but have observed, that some of those Pas-sages in this Discourse, which appear most liable to Objection are what they call Parodies, where the Author personates the Style and Manner of other Writers, whom he has a mind to expose. I shall produce one Instance, it is in the 51st Page. Dryden, L'Estrange, and some others I shall not name, are here levelled at, who having spent their Lives in Faction, and Apostacies, and all manner of Vice, pretended to be Sufferers for Loyalty and Religion. So Dryden tells us in one of his Prefaces of his Merits and Suffering, thanks God that he *possesses his Soul in Patience:* In other Places he talks at the same Rate, and L'Estrange often uses the like Style, and I believe the Reader may find more Persons to give that Passage an Application: But this is enough to direct those who may have over-look'd the Authors Intention.

As a sample of Dryden's complaints, I will quote a sentence from his *Discourse concerning Satire:*

29

But being encouraged only with fair words by King Charles II, my little salary ill paid, and no prospect of a future subsistence, I was then discouraged in the beginning of my attempt; and now age has overtaken me, and want, a more insufferable evil, through the change of the times, has wholly disenabled me.

But Dryden provided even better material in his translation of the *Works of Virgil*, which appeared in the summer of 1697, while Swift was probably working on the *Tale*. The volume was printed by Tonson in a handsome folio, adorned with a hundred sculptures, and a list of the names of the subscribers to the cuts, each subscription being five guineas; with a separate list of the second subscribers. It was divided into three parts, containing the Pastorals, the Georgics and the Aeneis, each part equipped not only with separate prefaces or observations, but also with separate dedications—to Lord Clifford, the Earl of Chesterfield and the Marquis of Normandy. Swift did not miss his opportunity:

Our famous Dryden has ventured to proceed a Point farther, endeavouring to introduce also a Multiplicity of God-fathers; which is an Improvement of much more Advantage, upon a very obvious Account.

It was such a good example that he would try it himself and therefore divided his treatise into forty

sections and approached forty Lords of his acquaintance to stand, but they all made their excuses.

But in the Postscript to the Reader, Swift found a
lovely sample of Dryden's further acknowledgments
to more god-fathers for all the encouragement and
aids he had received in the course of his work, start-
ing with the assistance granted by the Almighty in
the beginning, prosecution and conclusion of his
studies, and ending with his obligations to the whole
Faculty of medicine, especially to those two orna-
ments of their profession, Dr. Guibbons and Dr.
Hobbs. And finally he assures the reader that "His
work will be judged in after ages to be no dishonour
to his native country, whose language and poetry he
has added to in the choice of words and in the har-
mony of numbers." This Swift notes as an excellent
method of advertisement:

> Our great Dryden . . . has often said to me in
> Confidence, that the World would have never sus-
> pected him to be so great a Poet, if he had not
> assured them so frequently in his Prefaces, that
> it was impossible they could either doubt or for-
> get it.

Finally all such affectations as are found scattered
throughout these prefaces and addresses to the
reader, "all these wonderful civilities (as Swift calls
them) that have passed of late Years between the
Nation of Authors and that of Readers" are gath-

ered up in the extravagant travesty of one of the
final sections of the *Tale*, where the author offers his
humble thanks to his Majesty, and both Houses of
Parliament, the Lords of the Privy Council, the
Judges, clergy, gentry, and yeomanry of the land, etc.
for their approbation; expresses his happiness that
Fate has flung him into so blessed an age for the mutual felicity of authors and booksellers, who produce
and sell their wares so easily, and promises entire
satisfaction for every class of readers, the superficial,
the ignorant and the learned, and ends with throw-
ing out some bait for the latter group, by dropping
some dark hints and innuendoes of hidden meanings
and profound mysteries, in the hope—as the learned
commentator puts it in a final note—of setting curious men a-hunting through Indexes, and enquiring
for Books out of the common Road. I may add that
there are probably very few of us who have tried
to edit or comment on this *Tale*, who have not been
tricked in this manner, and I can only commend to
any of you who may be looking for a subject for research with unlimited possibilities, that you should
investigate the qualities of *Acamoth*, which you may,
or may not, find illuminated in the work of the dark
authors of the seventeenth century.

The method of parody is also used in the ridicule
of Bentley and Wotton, which occurs in the Digression on Critics when he sets out gravely to search

for particular descriptions of the True Critick in the writings of the Ancients, and brings together very much in the manner of Bentley a series of quotations proving that these Ancients generally fixed upon the same hieroglyph, as the subject was too dangerous to be treated except by types and figures. Thereupon the symbol of the ass is introduced with the help of two quotations from Pausanias. "But Herodotus, holding the very same Hieroglyph, speaks much plainer and almost *in terminis.* Upon which relation Ctesias yet refines, etc." And even the three Maxims which provide a devastating close for the chapter are ornamented with a number of similitudes, in which the prevalent witty conceit is sharpened so that it may become an effective weapon for satire. I will instance only the first of these where the irony is so nicely balanced that an early compositor added a negative which has confused the sentence as it now stands in many editions:

> Criticism, contrary to all other Faculties of the Intellect, is ever held the truest and best, when it is the very *first* Result of the Critick's Mind: As Fowlers reckon the first aim for the surest, and seldom fail of missing the Mark, if they stay for a Second.

I have spoken at such length about the parody in the book, because it explains its unlikeness to much of Swift's later work, and because it is, I think, the

source of that extraordinary richness and variety in
the style which is so much concerned with an examination of the books of the previous generation that
inevitably it preserves so many of their tricks and
mannerisms. But it contains also quite clearly and
fully developed the qualities also which most dis-
tinctively mark Swift's satire, "an Irony which runs
through the Thread of the whole Book" and a sar-
donic wit which is a perfect vehicle for a scepticism
not less profound and not less complete than that
which perhaps more plainly and nakedly reveals itself in his latest writings.

Consider for instance his answer to the problem
why satire is likely to be less dull than panegyrick.
The solution, he says, is easy and natural.

> For, the Materials of Panegyrick being very few
> in Number, have been long since exhausted: For,
> as Health is but one Thing and has been always
> the same, whereas Diseases are by thousands, be-
> sides new and daily Additions; So, all the virtues
> that have been ever in Mankind, are to be counted
> upon a few Fingers, but his Follies and Vices are
> innumerable, and Time adds hourly to the Heap.

That last phrase is so characteristic. It prevents the
sentence from falling flat, like some stale drab moralist's jibe. It thrusts it home, revealing the endless
possibility of mankind's follies mounting higher hour
by hour. It reminds us of the *Dedication to Prince*

34

*Posterity,* where beneath the gay raillery of his tone
as he bears witness to the actual reputation of his
illustrious contemporaries at the minute he is writing, there can be heard the theme of Time and Mor-
tality, and his sentences are caught for a moment
and held by that insistent rhythm which had been
dominant for a hundred years:

> I enquired after them among Readers and Book-
> sellers, but I enquired in vain, the Memorial of
> them was lost among Men, their Place was no
> more to be found; and I was laughed to scorn . . .

And then inexorably other echoes float into his mind
and bring him more images for his purpose, and, as
we read, his sentences are disturbed and rock a little
beneath the powerful swell of this very different
rhetoric:

> Sometime we see a cloud that's dragonish;
> A vapour sometime like a bear or lion,
> A tower'd citadel, a pendent rock,
> A forked mountain, or blue promontory
> With trees upon't, that nod unto the world,
> And mock our eyes with air: thou hast seen these
>     signs;
> They are black vesper's pageants.
> > > Ay, my lord.
> That which is now a horse, even with a thought
>     the rack dislimns.

Here is what Swift makes of it. I do not quote it as
an example of parody, but to show his mind in this

way also enriched by his reading, and subduing it
to his purpose.

> If I should venture in a windy Day, to affirm to
> Your Highness, that there is a large Cloud near the
> Horizon in the Form of a Bear, another in the
> Zenith with the Head of an Ass, a third to the west-
> ward with Claws like a Dragon; and Your High-
> ness should in a few Minutes think fit to examine
> the Truth, 'tis certain, they would all be changed
> in Figure and Position, new ones would arise, and
> all we could agree upon would be, that clouds
> there were, but that I was grossly mistaken in the
> *Zoography* and *Topography* of them.

Professor Sherburn has drawn attention to a
striking aspect of the *Tale,* often overlooked, as it
reveals Swift's "dislike of the deluding powers of
perverted reason," or, more specifically, his dislike
of proselytizing, of people who wish to force their
opinions upon others.

> Whoever hath *an Ambition to be heard in a Crowd*
> —so, with contempt, begins his Introduction to the
> *Tale;* and in the climactic Digression on Madness,
> the lunatics are the founders of states by conquest,
> the founders of new systems of philosophy, and the
> founders of sects in religion.

This is very true, but even in this there is an element
of irony, which I think Swift was not unaware of,
though it was at his own expense. For he also had
an ambition, and a very powerful ambition, to be

36

heard, and while he makes fun of those who exalt themselves above the crowd by mounting upon one of those three wooden machines for the use of orators who desire to talk much without interruption, he has nevertheless devised his own Tub to provide a platform for his own special wit and genius. And it cannot be denied that he has sometimes endeavoured to satisfy the "Whale-mouthed gapers after Levity," and has taken advantage of "the liberty of these Times, which hath afforded Wisdom a larger Passport to travel, than was ever able formerly to be obtained, when the World kept her fettered in an implicite Obedience, by the three-fold Cord of Custom, Education and Ignorance." Even when Swift is most directly attacking the sects, and may be in part influenced by his own experience among the Presbyterians in Ireland, he is still writing not as a churchman or a politician, but as a wit and as a man of letters. That is perhaps the fundamental difference between the *Tale* and the roughest controversial satires of the bishops and their opponents. They are always at certain points protected and restrained by their official status. But the author of the *Tale* is completely free, unhampered by political or practical considerations. He is concerned with words; his wit is conceit; and he did not always realize perhaps the power and the effect of the weapons he was using.

In his handling of the allegory of the three brothers, for instance, he is inclined to dramatize their actions rather in the manner of the contemporary stage, and their language and gestures remind us of the world of Sir Novelty Fashion and Lord Foppington. And the symbol of the coats, meaning "the Doctrine and Faith of Christianity," is full of obvious dangers, though it not only lends itself to the necessary dramatization but also may be neatly reversed and elaborated into a satire on the real religion of the fashionable world, its god the tailor, and its system of belief according to which the universe is a large suit of Clothes and man himself but a micro-Coat, the acquirements of his mind furnishing an exact dress:

> Is not Religion a Cloak, Honesty a Pair of Shoes, worn out in the Dirt, Self-Love a Surtout, Vanity a Shirt, and Conscience a Pair of Breeches?

The whole of this passage is like a string of puns and conceits held together by a thread of irony. The dangers of Swift's satire on the corruptions of religion, whether in the allegory itself, or in the account of the sect of the Aeolists and the Fragment on the mechanical operation of the Spirit, arise out of the verbal play of his wit, which does not hesitate to make a sort of punning game with all the words which had become, it is true, soiled and bent by the usage they had received at the hands of hypocrites and fanatics, but which had nevertheless also been upon the lips of saints and prophets and remained for the devout Christian sacred symbols of his faith. It is not merely that the book contains "several youthful Sallies," or that "no one Opinion can fairly be deduced from it, which is contrary to Religion or Morality"—it is rather that the Author of *A Tale of a Tub* with an audience of "the greatest Droles and Wits that any Age ever produced," set out to establish his reputation among them by outdistancing them all in the variety of his drollery and the reach and penetration of his wit.

In this he succeeded. None of them went farther in their probing, none of them journeyed farther in the exploration of a rationalist's complete scepticism, none of them opened their minds so freely and without prejudice to all that was being thought and said, none of them—not even Sir Thomas Browne— more eloquently expressed that experience of following the mind of man through all its magnificent and fantastic vagaries during the century. Here Swift shows what he could have done, had he wished to write like them. Here is a tour de force, a superb imitation of their most exalted rhetorical periods, soaring into the empyrean in circling parodies of their favourite cosmic images, only to burst at last into an explosive flash of wit, as he compares man's fancy to the brightly plumaged bird of paradise that was reputed to live only in the heights of the air.

39

AND, whereas the mind of Man, when he gives the Spur and Bridle to his Thoughts, doth never stop, but naturally sallies out into both extreams of High and Low, of Good and Evil; His first Flight of Fancy, commonly transports Him to Idea's of what is most Perfect, finished, and exalted; till having soared out of his own Reach and Sight, not well perceiving how near the Frontiers of Height and Depth, border upon each other; With the same Course and Wing, he falls down plum into the lowest Bottom of Things; like one who travels the East into the West; or like a strait Line drawn by its own length into a Circle. Whether a Tincture of Malice in our Natures, makes us fond of furnishing every bright Idea with its Reverse; Or, whether Reason reflecting upon the Sum of Things, can, like the Sun, serve only to enlighten one half of the Globe, leaving the other half, by Necessity, under Shade and Darkness: Or, whether Fancy, flying up to the imagination of what is Highest and Best, becomes over-short, and spent, and weary, and suddenly falls like a dead Bird of Paradise, to the Ground.

But no one has more lightly tossed aside these metaphysical conjectures to argue triumphantly in the cause of reason and common sense, ironically exposing the delusions of the imagination, and the dangers of all philosophical anatomizing, and showing the wisdom of contenting ourselves with the superficies of things, only to bring us to this conclusion:

40

This is the sublime and refined Point of Felicity, called, *The Possession of being well* deceived; the Serene, Peaceful State of being a Fool among Knaves.

And no one has gone quite so far—not even that "absolute Lord of Wit," the Earl of Rochester, who was indeed quite unhampered in his profanity and little concerned with man's dignity—as the Author of *A Tale of a Tub* when he recommends as a very noble undertaking to Tory members of the House of Commons that they should appoint a commission (who shall be empowered to send for Persons, Papers, and Records) to examine into the merits of every student and professor in Bedlam, so that they might be properly used for all the offices in the state, ecclesiastical, civil and military. Various suitable candidates are vividly described and their special fitness for various occupations indicated; and the irony is pressed home in a characteristically thorough manner, by the evident manifestation that "all would very much excel, and arrive at great Perfection in their several Kinds." In case anyone should doubt this, the author of these momentous truths modestly claims to have had the happiness of being for some time a worthy member of that honourable society, and by that one plain instance clinches his argument, admitting gravely that he is "a Person, whose Imaginations are hard-mouth'd, and exceedingly disposed to run away with his *Reason*," which he had observed "from long experience, to be a very light Rider, and easily shook off."

Dr. Johnson relates that "when this wild work first raised the attention of the publick, Sacheverell, meeting Smalridge, tried to flatter him by seeming to think him the author; but Smalridge answered with indignation, 'Not all that you and I have in the world nor all that ever we shall have, should hire me to write the *Tale of a Tub*.'" Perhaps there is some reason for such an attitude, not because the *Tale* is sometimes unconventional, or even profane; but because it reveals so fully through all the parody and wit and irony the intellectual experience of the author. Though there were chasms in the manuscript, where we are told certain passages were omitted, the book as printed gives the impression of holding nothing back. It is in the tradition of the century that was closing as it was written; it is in the direct line of Wit, and it may not be altogether extravagant to say that it makes an effective epilogue, and leaves the stage clear for a new and rather different set of actors. And perhaps it almost meets on a different level the requirements of one of the most notable wits in the company for whom Swift wrote, the Duke of Buckingham, who at the end of the century challenged his generation to produce another writer of such sincerity, as he who from the beginning of the century had exercised so much influence in England,—the incomparable Montaigne. "Yet," he says, "whenever any great Wit shall incline to the same free way of writing, I almost dare assure him of success; for besides the agreeableness of such a book, so very sincere a temper of mind needs not blush to be exposed as naked as possible." I venture to shock you by linking Montaigne and Swift together and to recommend to you the reading of *A Tale of a Tub,* not only because it is a very entertaining and a very witty book, but because it reveals as nakedly and as fearlessly as possible the intellectual experience of a man of letters, who had reached the age of thirty a little before the turn of the century together with what might not too fancifully be called the first generation of the modern world.

## II

## POLITICAL SATIRE

He was an *honest man* I'll swear—:
Why Sir, I differ from you there,
For, I have heard another Story,
He was a most *confounded Tory—!*

IN EXAMINING Swift's political satire we shall be concerned mainly with his writings during two periods of four years; the first, when he wrote for the Tory Ministry of the last four years of Queen Anne's reign, for an English audience in London under the name of "Examiner"; and the second, when he wrote for an Irish audience in Dublin, particularly from 1720 to 1724, when he assumed the name and manner of a Dublin linen draper, though he continued later after his last visit to England in 1727 from time to time to play a part in Irish affairs.

Swift was of course no stranger to the world of politics before he entered the service of the Tories. As secretary to Sir William Temple and as editor of his works, he had been at a point of vantage to observe the course of affairs since the Revolution; and the first printed work of which he was proud, though rather an academic performance, received great approbation, and brought him as soon as he was known to be the author the acquaintance of Lord Somers and Lord Halifax. But the best account of this is provided by Swift himself in his *Memoirs relating to that change in the Queen's Ministry in 1710:*

Although I had been for many years before no stranger to the court, and had made the nature of government a great part of my study, yet I had dealt very little with politics, either in writing or acting, till about a year before the late *King William's* death; when, returning with the Earl of Berkeley from Ireland, and falling upon the subject of the five great lords who were then impeached, for high crimes and misdemeanours, by the House of Commons, I happened to say, 'That the same manner of proceeding, at least as it appeared to me from the views we received from it in Ireland, had ruined the liberties of Athens and Rome; and that it might be easy to prove it from history.' Soon after I went to London; and, in a few weeks, drew up a discourse, under the title of *The Contests and Dissensions of the Nobles and Commons in Athens and Rome, with the Consequences they had upon both those States.*
. . . I soon grew domestic with Lord Halifax and was as often with Lord Somers as the formality of his nature (the only unconversable fault he has) made it agreeable to me.
It was then I first began to trouble myself with the difference between the principles of Whig and Tory; having formerly employed myself in other, and I think much better speculations. I talked often upon this subject with Lord Somers; told him, that, having been long conversant with the

Greek and Roman authors, and therefore a lover of liberty, I found myself much inclined to be what they called a Whig in politics; and that, besides, I thought it impossible, upon any other principle, to defend, or submit to, the Revolution; but, as to religion, I confessed myself to be a high churchman, and that I did not conceive how any one, who wore the habit of a clergyman, could be otherwise.

He then goes on to point to the pamphlets he had written two years before he was first introduced to Harley, in which he had opposed the party then in power and, in particular, had written against the measures which it was expected the Earl of Wharton would undertake to get the Sacramental Test removed in Ireland. But the first three of these tracts are hardly political satire; two of them indeed seem to have been written for the volume of *Miscellanies* which did not eventually appear until 1711. In *The Sentiments of a Church-of-England Man with Respect to Religion and Government* he definitely proposes to write in such a way as would be liable to the least objection from either party; he satirizes only the spirit of faction and recommends to those who desire "to preserve the Constitution entire in Church and State . . . to avoid the Extreams of *Whig* for the Sake of the former, and the Extreams of *Tory* on Account of the latter." And in the *Argument*

49

*against Abolishing Christianity* he writes still in the character of a Wit and a young gentleman much in the world and therefore needing to rely wholly on irony to uphold such an unpopular cause as the Established Church, against the arguments of the free-thinkers and the men of pleasure and the politicians who are all bent upon its destruction. There are many passages which remind us of *A Tale of a Tub*, for instance:

> There is a Portion of Enthusiasm assigned to every Nation, which if it hath not proper Objects to work on, will burst out, and set all in a Flame. If the Quiet of a State can be bought by only flinging Men a few Ceremonies to devour, it is a Purchase no wise Man would refuse. Let the Mastiffs amuse themselves about a Sheep-skin stuffed with Hay, provided it will keep them from worrying the Flock.

I would almost say that it is written with such enjoyment of the play of irony, and with such an indulgence in wit, or on the other hand, with such contempt of the ways of the world, and occasionally with such double-edged scorn, that it hardly succeeds in its defence of the Establishment or in its support of the dignity of the clergy, "who are the only great Restorers of our Breed"; having been "reduced by the wise Regulations of Henry the Eighth, to the Necessity of a low Diet, and moderate Exercise." And even that Tory tract, the *Project for the Advancement of Religion* addressed to the Countess of Berkeley, and printed in 1709, though advocating that the Court should exert its full authority and employ in the government and the offices of State only orthodox members of the Church party, was so clothed in the language of morality that a good Whig like Steele took occasion to commend it highly in the *Tatler*.

But in the other tract that Swift later mentions with justifiable pride as a proof of his attitude while the Whigs were still in power, which appeared as *A Letter from a Member of the House of Commons of Ireland concerning the Sacramental Test*, he appears for the first time in action as a political satirist, writing on a specific matter on behalf of the High-Church party and at the same time in his impersonation of an Irish M.P., surprising us by a curious foreshadowing of his later role as a Hibernian patriot. Here already is that fierce indignation, strengthened by the double force of his feelings *for* Ireland and *against* an English policy he hated on its own account. Often—he says—since he had read Cowley's Love Verses at the age of fifteen, he had imagined these lines to be spoken by Ireland:

> Forbid it Heaven my Life should be
> Weigh'd with her least Conveniency.

If your little Finger be sore, and you think a Poul-

tice made of our *Vitals* will give it any Ease, speak
the Word, and it shall be done;

The pamphlet was written as a warning against the
designs of which the Earl of Wharton was suspected
to get the Test Act first repealed in Ireland; and it
bore also the weight of Swift's personal dislike, since
Wharton had received him so coldly over the matter of remitting the First Fruits to the Irish clergy,
and had appointed Lambert, a Whig Low-Church-
man, to be his chaplain. During the course of his
government in Ireland, Swift remained aloof, and
his dislike of Wharton turned to distrust and hatred
and contempt, which found expression in a violent
attack, dated from London, August 30, 1710, and
entitled *A short Character of his Excellency Thomas
Earl of Wharton, Lord Lieutenant of Ireland.*

In all his political satire in both England and Ireland Swift made full use of his personal dislikes to
destroy the public reputation of the leaders of the
opposing party. His method is to adopt the role of a
cold impartial examiner, patiently and thoroughly
exposing the wretched and corrupt state of his victims in a mood which reminds us of the remark of
the author of *A Tale of a Tub*, when he is warning
us against the danger of anatomizing: "Last Week
I saw a Woman flay'd, and you will hardly believe,
how much it altered her Person for the worse." In
the process of his examining of Thomas, Earl of

Wharton, he confesses that he enters on the work
with more cheerfulness because it is not possible to
make him angry or hurt his reputation, as he is
entirely without the sense of shame or glory; and
then with considerable precision he delineates the
character of an unscrupulous, intriguing, lying, foul-
mouthed politician driven by three predominant
passions not usually found together, "Love of
Power, Love of Money, and Love of Pleasure, but
since he went to Ireland . . . most disposed to the
second . . . having gained by his Government of
under two Years, five and forty thousand Pounds by
the most favourable Computation, half in the regular Way, and half in the prudential."

But it was even more important in the interest of
the Queen and her new ministers to strike at the
powerful group they had supplanted by under-
mining the reputation of the great general himself.
Swift did not hesitate before the difficulty of such
a task, or allow his private opinions to modify the
force of those arguments which were necessary to
justify the action taken by the Ministry in setting
aside the Duke. In the *Journal to Stella* for January
1, 1712, he tells her that he had dined with the
Secretary,

> and it is true that the Duke of Marlborough is
> turned out of all. . . . If the Ministry be not sure
> of a peace, I shall wonder at this step, and do not

approve it at best. . . . however it be, the world abroad will blame us. I confess my belief that he has not one good quality in the world beside that of a general, and even that I have heard denied by several great soldiers. But we have had constant success in arms while he commanded. Opinion is a mighty matter in war, and I doubt the French think it impossible to conquer an army that he leads, and our soldiers think the same; and how far even this step may encourage the French to play tricks with us, no man knows. I do not love to see personal resentment mix with public affairs.

Nevertheless, once the step had been taken, it was his duty to justify it thoroughly in order to prepare the way for a peace with France by discrediting Marlborough's later handling of the campaign in the Netherlands. The main argument is that England ought not to have committed herself so deeply to support the Dutch by land, but should have taken the opportunity to build up her own sea power and impoverish France and Spain by attacks on their shipping and colonies. But unfortunately the sea was not the Duke of Marlborough's element, and such a plan would not have contributed to his prestige and profit.

And further he does not hesitate to follow the method which he had proved and continued to use in all controversies, the method which he frankly described in this simple formula:

In all Contests the safest way is to put those we dispute with as much *in the Wrong* as we can.

So, a month later, he set to work to put Marlborough as much in the wrong as he could, by exposing his two weaknesses—his ambition, which led him to ask to be made general for life, and his avarice, which Swift deals with so subtly in his *Letter to Marcus Crassus,* published in the *Examiner,* February 8, 1710-11. It is a masterpiece of detraction, masked with opening phrases of compliment and genuine praise of the great qualities of the general which lead naturally to the question why he has not gained the love of the army abroad or the people at home. This is because, though he is the richest person in the land, he is "deeply stained with that odious and ignoble Vice of *Covetousness.*" "If he does not believe it let him disguise himself and go among his soldiers and among the common people and listen to what they say about him; or let him ask his own nearest friends." And then the epistle concludes with this neat sentence:

The moment you quit this Vice, you will be a truly Great Man; and still there will Imperfections enough remain to convince us, you are not a *God.* Farewell.

It would be tempting to quote the satirical Elegy that Swift wrote at the time of Marlborough's death;

55

but that was too late to be of any use as political satire. It indicates however something rather significant in Swift's own conception of himself as an impartial examiner; he seems so sure of himself in that role that he wished also to be the historiographer of the time, officially appointed to provide a true and impartial record for posterity. It was this that led him to pursue his enemies beyond the grave, so that the evil they committed would still stand as a judgment against them, or as he pleasantly puts it in justifying his attack later on the Lord Chief Justice of Ireland:

> It is certain that people distinguished for their villainy have as good a title for a blast from the proper trumpet, (of fame) as those who are most renowned for their virtues from the other; and have equal reason to complain if it be refused them.

Certainly Swift undertook this double duty in the *Examiner*, a paper which the ministry had launched "to provide just reflections upon former proceedings and defend the present measures of her Majesty." Bolingbroke, Atterbury, Prior and a few friends were responsible for it at first, but Harley proposed to Swift that he should take it over entirely, and seems to have made some promise that he should be established in England. Thus for about eight months he wrote these weekly papers entirely himself, from the beginning of November 1710 to the middle of June 1711.

By the end of the eight months he could boast that his work was done, "the main body of the Whigs entirely subdued, and that there only remained to be dealt with a few wretches who had nothing left but their bare good will towards Faction and Mischief." And as far as he was concerned they could be disposed of in a final conceit:

> For my own particular, those little barking Pens which have so constantly pursued me, I take to be of no further Consequence to what I have writ, than the scoffing Slaves of old, placed behind the Chariot, to put the General in Mind of his Mortality; which was but a Thing of Form, and made no Stop or Disturbance in the Show. However, if those perpetual Snarlers against me had the same Design, I must own they have effectually compassed it; since nothing can well be more mortifying, than to reflect, that I am of the same Species with Creatures capable of uttering so much Scurrility, Dulness, Falshood and Impertinence, to the Scandal and Disgrace of Human Nature.

He had throughout his campaign taken every opportunity to dissociate himself from these mere party hacks by maintaining a middle ground between the High-fliers and the Dissenters, between the *Rehearsal* and the *Medley;* and he had frequently tried

57

to expose the use of "the cant-words, Whig and Tory," which had so often varied their significance in their thirty years' history, and to prove that the new ministry had wide-spread and national support, while their opponents were a mixture of heterogeneous factions which could not conceivably be brought together in the unity of a single party.

As I believe I may possibly assume that these *Examiner* papers are not often carefully studied except by those who are concerned with the political history of this period, I shall draw your attention more particularly to No. 34, dated March 29, 1711, in which Swift very simply and clearly exposes the method of his irony. We can observe his success in using it as a device to convince his readers of the reasonableness of his own middle position, as a fair impartial examiner, who was completely protected against his opponents from either extreme. It is a device which can be recommended in political debate, because it works by a process of simplification, setting over against one another certain antithetical ideas and propositions, and breaking down the whole complicated pattern into a few plain figures in black and white, which can be easily brought together for comparison and contrast.

In this paper he begins by confessing that he has grown weary of the job of examining and has therefore been led to take stock of his position, and to consider what would become of him, *if Times should alter;* but after mature consideration he decides that there is no cause for anxiety:

> what I have said on Occasion, concerning the late Men in Power, may be called Satyr by some unthinking People, as long as that Faction is down; but if ever they come into Play again I must give them warning beforehand, that I shall expect to be a *Favourite,* and that those pretended Advocates of theirs, will be Pilloried for *Libellers.*

In like manner he had imagined that he had been complimenting the present ministry, when he had spoken of their loyalty to the Queen and the old constitution in Church and State, and their desire for an honourable peace.

> But it seems I am mistaken, and they reckon all this for Satyr, because it is directly contrary to the Practice of all those whom they set up to defend, and utterly against all their Notions of a good Ministry. Therefore I cannot but think they have Reason on their side: For, suppose I should write the Character of an Honest, a Religious, and a learned Man, and send the first to *Newgate,* and the second to the *Grecian Coffee-House,* and the last to *White's;* would they not all pass for *Satyrs,* and justly enough, among the Companies to whom they were sent?
>
> Having therefore employed several Papers in such sort of *Panegyricks,* and but very few on what they understand to be *Satyrs;* I shall henceforth

upon Occasion be more Liberal of the latter; of which they are like to have a Taste in the remainder of this present Paper.

He can appeal to the simple irony in the situation to justify his examination of the facts; he is as impartial as the Recording Angel; it is but calling things by different names—panegyric or satire—and both parties equally approve, and applaud his excellent strokes. It is a neatly balanced performance which cannot be upset within the limits of the stage he has arranged. And the argument is so strongly woven that there is nothing to get hold of and twist out of shape. As a political satirist he is always concerned to rally his supporters, and to over-run all opposition, never to win over his opponents by persuasion or by concession. He has nothing of the temper of that real exponent of the via media, and Trimmer, the Marquis of Halifax; and though he was "for some time domesticate with him," shows little of his influence, none of his wise caution and scepticism, when he gives advice on the way to handle a political argument:

there is hardly a single Proposition to be made, which is not deceitful, and the tying our Reason too close to it, may in many Cases be destructive. Circumstances must come in, and are to be made a part of the Matter of which we are to judge; positive Decisions are always dangerous, more es-

pecially in *Politicks*. A Man, who will be a Master
of an Argument, must do like a skilful General,
who sendeth Scouts on all sides, to see whether
there may not be an Enemy. So he must look
round to see what Objections can be made, and
not go in a straight Line, which is the ready way
to lead him into a mistake.

Swift never looks round, or lets us look round if
he can help it, to see what objections can be made,
and he always prefers to move in a straight line, attacking directly straight down the middle, dividing
his enemies to the left and to the right, passing
through them unharmed and leaving them to their
mutual destruction. And he would doubtless retort
that it was not his fault if events within a very few
years turned some of the *Examiner's* compliments to
the new ministry and the new parliament into very
bitter satire indeed.

Meantime he continued to provide the ministry
with clear statements confidently justifying their
policy in a series of pamphlets designed to win approval for the conclusion of a peace with France—
*The Conduct of the Allies, The Barrier Treaty*, etc.
That was his most dignified and important role, for
he contributed a clear and reasonable analysis of the
situation, which had immediate effect in producing
the necessary change of opinion both in the House
of Commons and in the country. Again in these

pamphlets he assumes with extraordinary conviction his role as impartial Examiner, though he trusts in fact to his favourite method of detraction, of proving in the wrong the Whig ministers who had bribed the Dutch to continue the war by offering them all the advantages of the Barrier Treaty instead of taking the perfect opportunity which had been presented them to make a completely satisfactory peace for Europe. Similarly he exposes the short-sightedness and selfishness of the Dutch in using the position for their own benefit, and so convincingly proves them in the wrong that he almost seems to justify the dishonourable betrayal of their Allies which the Tory ministry was actually planning. And finally he attempts to discredit them both—the Whigs and the Dutch alike—as belonging to a solemn League and Covenant devoted to their own base interests at the expense of the true welfare of the people of England:

I have here imputed the Continuance of the War to the mutual Indulgence between our General and Allies, wherein they both so well found their Accounts; to the Fears of the *Money-changers,* lest their *Tables should be overthrown;* to the Designs of the Whigs, who apprehended the Loss of their Credit and Employments in a Peace; and to those at home, who held their immoderate Engrossments of Power and Favour, by no other Tenure, than their own Presumption upon the Necessity of Affairs. The Truth of this will appear indisputable, by considering with what Unanimity and Concert these several Parties acted towards that great End.

At the same time, he did not neglect other levels of attack, coming to the relief of the ministry with a squib giving a mock account of Prior's journey to Paris when that diplomatic secret mission was prematurely discovered, tossing hints to his aides and assistants in party journalism, and putting out ballads and popular verses against the Earl of Nottingham and the Duchess of Somerset, or the Duke of Marlborough. They were usually tried out first for the private amusement of the Brothers Society, and then, if approved, printed off on a half sheet the next day for the benefit of the public. In the pages of the *Journal to Stella,* we can watch him triumphantly at work, enjoying the excitement of public life and the invigorating experience of success in political action, seeing the results of his skilful plans. But before the death of the Queen—after his return from Dublin when he was installed as Dean in 1713, the growing division in the Ministry made it impossible for him to help them any longer:

> By Faction tir'd, with Grief he waits awhile,
> His great contending Friends to reconcile.
> Performs what Friendship, Justice, Truth require:
> What could he more, but decently retire?

His retirement from active politics was to last for six years. During that time he was to write only memoirs, histories and verses—'all Panegyricks.' But in a letter addressed to Charles Ford, in December 1719, there is a strong hint that this period of inaction is nearly over.

> . . . as the World is now turned, no Cloyster is retired enough to keep Politicks out, . . .

There was indeed noise enough that winter in Dublin to disturb Swift in the corner of his Deanery, and when in March 1720 the *Act for the better securing the Dependency of the Kingdom of Ireland upon the Crown of Great Britain* was passed, taking away the jurisdiction of the Irish House of Lords, the general discontent spread to all parties.

> I do assure you I never saw so universall a Discontent as there is among the highest most virulent and anti-church Whigs against that Bill and every Author or Abetter of it without Exception. They say publickly that having been the most loyall submissive complying Subjects that ever Prince had, no Subjects were ever so ill treated.

Swift's comment shows the fundamental position he took throughout in all his activities as the Dublin linen draper: "The Question is whether People ought to be Slaves or no."

In all his writings concerning Irish politics his object was to prevent collaboration and to keep

64

alive the spirit of independence which would resist
by every possible means all further encroachments
of the British government in London on the liberties of Ireland. He could not hope to do much with
the leaders of the Church in Ireland or the men in
public employment, because they were appointed
by the Crown or under the influence of the Lord
Lieutenant; therefore, his only chance was to rouse
a popular campaign among the shopkeepers and
country people of Ireland.

He began his campaign with a Proposal for the
universal use of Irish Manufacture, in clothes, and
furniture of Houses, etc., utterly rejecting and re-
nouncing everything wearable that comes from England. This appeal to the public to boycott all goods
from England, or as he put it in the popular phrase
of the moment, "to burn everything that comes from
England except their people and their coal," was
printed in Dublin just before the celebrations arranged for May 28, 1720, in honour of the sixtieth
birthday of King George. Though it is written with
wit and humour, and though he attacks the Irish
Parliament for their neglect of the state of the nation and the shopkeepers for their lack of common
sense, though he adds a final word of contempt for
the project of a Bank in Dublin, his main purpose
was perfectly clear—to attack again his old political
enemies, the Whig ministers and the moneyed men,

to rouse the feelings of the Irish people against them, and stir their resentment against them on account of the universal oppression which was evident throughout the whole land.

Like all his Irish Tracts, this was no mere literary production—it was political satire and political action; and it brought Swift into conflict with the Lord Chancellor and with the Chief Justice of Ireland. The printer was brought to trial immediately, and the Chief Justice did his utmost to get him convicted, sending back the jury nine times, and finally postponing the case until the next term. Swift was able to get the matter settled by using the influence of his friends in England upon the Duke of Grafton, the Lord Lieutenant, but he never forgave Whitshed, whom he was to meet again and to defeat on a more serious occasion.

Although this proposal for a boycott did not have any direct result, Swift adopted the same tactics four years later to meet another questionable project in English dealings with the people of Ireland. In 1722 a certain William Wood obtained a patent to coin and send into Ireland a limited amount of copper coinage. In spite of immediate protests against the patent from the Commissioners of the Revenue in Dublin, agreements were quietly made in 1723 for the delivery of the first consignments of the copper coins to Ireland. This aroused

violent opposition, and, soon after the arrival of the
Duke of Grafton as Lord Lieutenant in August of
that year, both houses of Parliament drew up Addresses condemning the patent. This forced the
British government to order an enquiry in the
spring of 1724. At this moment Swift took action by
printing *A Letter to the Shopkeepers, Tradesmen,
Farmers and Common People of Ireland* by M. B.
Drapier, in the form of a penny pamphlet, copies
of which were available for distribution at a special
rate of three dozen for two shillings.

This was the first of the series of letters which
appeared during the year 1724, when Swift happened to be kept in Dublin throughout the summer
because he was building a wall round part of his
property, and so as it were by chance became involved in this episode of Wood's copper coinage.
These letters were not, however, mere bagatelles
for the amusement of the Dean and his friends,
though they doubtless served that purpose excel-
lently. But again they were a form of direct political action just the same as if he had gone out into
the streets and addressed the people. They were
written with the single purpose of persuading the
people of Ireland to boycott Wood's coinage, and
force the Crown to cancel the patent.

He had pointed out in his *Letter to a young
Clergyman* in 1720 that the constant design of the

great orators of Greece and Rome in all their speeches "was to drive some one particular point, either the condemnation or acquittal of an accused person; a persuasive to war, the enforcing of a law, and the like: which was determined on the spot, according as the orators on either side prevailed." And he had there expressed his preference for the method of Demosthenes, who relied on the strength of his arguments offered to the understanding and the reason. But his Dublin audience was a simple one, and the formal methods of oratory were not to his taste; so he translates his argument into the plain unlearned speech that might be supposed to to be the voice of a linen draper of Dublin. Yet through the mask he is careful that you should, if you are clever enough, recognize who is speaking. The opening sentences of Letter I, to readers in Dublin in March 1724, would, I think, at once be recognizable as having the tone which they were accustomed to hear from the pulpit of St. Patrick's. And as if to make sure of this he associates himself on the very next page with the *Proposal,* that had appeared four years earlier, which in Dublin was certainly known to have been written by him. The rest of the Letter is a plain statement of facts about the proposed coinage, and the laws governing coinage, which justified the rejection of Wood's copper —ending with an argument very direct in its appeal:

"Any person may expect to get a Quart of Two Penny Ale for Thirty-six of them."

The second letter did not appear until August, when the rumours of the new modified proposal began to appear in the newspapers. It ended with a sample Declaration against Wood's coinage which Swift proposed should be signed by two or three hundred leading gentlemen of the Kingdom. The third followed shortly after, as soon as the Report of the Committee was published. These letters contain an attack on the London Committee's enquiry, a close examination of their Report, and are enlivened by some of Swift's best invective against Mr. Wood and indirectly against Walpole.

> And he defied the Armies of the Living God. Goliah's Conditions of Combat were likewise the same with those of Wood. If he prevail against us, then shall we be his Servants: But if it happen that I prevail over him, I renounce the other part of the Condition, he shall never be a Servant of Mine, for I do not think him fit to be Trusted in any Honest Man's Shop.

He then proceeds to outline a plan for carrying out the boycott:

i. Declarations against Wood's coinage by all public bodies and by all tradesmen.
ii. A boycott of all tradesmen who should accept the coin.

There remained however the danger that as soon as the new Lord Lieutenant should arrive, he would succeed by the usual bribery and pressure in winning over the influential people to back the scheme. Swift therefore prepared another letter, this time addressed to the whole People of Ireland, and got it printed ready for circulation in the streets of Dublin on the very day that Carteret landed.

Here his method is entirely different. This is not the time for invective, and Lord Carteret for whom he had great admiration could not be attacked. Instead of that, he meets him with compliments and at the same time takes care very subtly to warn the Irish leaders against the sort of methods that might be employed to win them over. He reminds them that, however liable to temptation they may be, Lord Carteret has really very little to tempt them with, as all the good posts in the government were already given to Englishmen. But the real sting of the pamphlet was to be found in the passage dealing with the question of Ireland's dependence upon England.

I have looked over all the English and Irish Statutes without finding any Law that makes Ireland depend upon England, any more than England does upon Ireland. We have indeed obliged our selves to have the same King with them, and consequently they are obliged to have the same King with us. For the Law was made by our own Parliament, and our Ancestors then were not such Fools (whatever they were in the Preceding Reign) to bring themselves under I know not what Dependance, which is now talked of without any Ground of Law, Reason or Common Sense.

Let whoever think otherwise, I M. B. Drapier, desire to be excepted, for I declare, next under God, I depend only on the King my Sovereign, and on the Laws of my own Country; and I am so far from depending upon the People of England, that if they should ever Rebel against my Sovereign (which God forbid) I would be ready at the first Command from his Majesty to take Arms against them, as some of my Country-men did against Theirs at Preston. And if such a Rebellion should prove so successful as to fix the Pretender on the Throne of England, I would venture to transgress that Statute so far as to lose every Drop of my Blood to hinder him from being King of Ireland.

This was going very near to high treason. Carteret took immediate action, by calling the Privy Council together, and persuading them to offer a reward of £300 for the discovery of the author, and to arrest the printer. It was a comic situation, for he and everyone else at the Castle knew pretty well who the author was. And for a time Swift apparently thought of coming forward and challenging the authorities to arrest him. He was probably advised not to do this.

The declarations continued to come in and the whole business of Parliament was held up. When the case of the printer came before the Grand Jury, Swift put out a paper giving them advice how to act and attacking Whitshed; and when this was also proceeded against, he provided them with a declaration, which was read out in court to the scandal of the judges, in which they used the opportunity of declaring their opposition to Wood instead of proceeding against Swift's printer. Verses were hawked in the streets against the Chief Justice, and the people of Dublin repeated the words of the Book of Samuel.

> And the people said unto Saul, Shall Jonathan die, who hath wrought this great salvation in Israel? God forbid: as the Lord liveth, there shall not one hair of his head fall to the ground, for he hath wrought with God this day. So the people rescued Jonathan, that he died not.

Carteret saw that nothing could be done, and in due time on his advice the patent was withdrawn. In the meantime Swift published another letter addressed to an enlightened liberal peer, Lord Molesworth, in which with gentle irony he reviews the course of the whole controversy and his part in it, using the terms of his own trade as a draper. It is perhaps the wittiest of the letters, published at a time when it was no longer necessary for him to use his more powerful weapons. There is a sort of triumphant gaiety about it, fitting the mood of a Dublin which began to believe in the success of the opposition they had made, and was inclined to enjoy the fun of it. But it was also important in the campaign—he might have gone too far. It contained also an appeal from the Dean to other Dublin leaders to stand by him.

It is surprisingly exciting to read the official documents of the time as they were sent in by all sorts of different people to London, reporting each new surprise, as it took place. It was indeed not Swift alone who enjoyed the situation; the venerable Archbishop of Dublin made the most of it also in the House of Lords, carrying it to a fine finish, even after the patent was withdrawn, and when their Lordships were drawing up an address of thanks to his Majesty for his favour to them. He cleverly inserted in the Address the words *in his great wisdom* referring to his Majesty's withdrawal of the patent, and when it was accepted was heard to say with great satisfaction, that that would indicate that it was anything but great wisdom to have granted it in the first place. Whereupon the innuendo was noticed and the House of Lords debated the phrase for two days much to the enjoyment of Dublin.

Swift had prepared a final letter to the Irish Parliament to be ready for their opening, but when the news came of the withdrawal of the patent he wrote immediately to his friends to stop the printing:

> . . . Since Wood's patent is cancelled, it will by no means be convenient to have the paper printed, as I suppose you, and Jack Grattan, and Sheridan will agree; therefore if it be with the printer, I would have it taken back, and the press broke, and let her be satisfied. The work is done, and there is no more need of the Drapier.

He had written to get something done, not to show off his wit or amuse an audience. Therefore when the thing was done, the desired result obtained, there was no further need that what he had written should be read.

He continued to interest himself in the affairs of Ireland, however, and in 1727 seems to have hoped that in the new reign there might be some improvement. He even went to the trouble of explaining the needs of that wretched country to Walpole. But when nothing came of this direct effort, and when his continued warnings, even in Ireland, were unheeded, he abandoned political action and turned to irony and the satisfaction of personal invective in his verses against both Walpole and the Parliament in Dublin. And finally, when the Duke of Dorset came over as Lord Lieutenant to Ireland in the fall of 1731, Swift assured him that he need

have no anxiety that the Drapier would cause him
the least inconvenience during his term of office. I
quote his own words from a letter to the Countess
of Suffolk, October 1731:

> If any state scribble writ here should happen to
> reach London, I entreat your Ladyship would
> continue to do me the justice of believing my inno-
> cence, because I lately assured the Duke of Dorset
> that I would never have a hand in any such thing,
> and I gave him my reason before his Secretary,
> that looking upon this kingdom's condition as ab-
> solutely desperate, I would not prescribe a dose
> to the dead.

# III

## MORAL SATIRE

Sir, our *Accounts* are diff'rent quite,
And your *Conjectures* are not right;
'Tis plain, his Writings were design'd
To please, and to reform Mankind;
And, if he often miss'd his Aim,
The *World* must own it, to their *shame;*
The *Praise* is *His,* and *Theirs* the *Blame.*

I HAVE TRIED in these lectures on Swift's satire so far to examine his method, first, as he was concerned with the world of letters, the Author of *A Tale of a Tub*, writing as a wit with his reading fresh in his head, so that the result is very literary, full of parody and of echoes of seventeenth century literature; and second, as he was concerned with the world of politics, both in London and in Dublin, when he appeared in the role of Tory Examiner and Drapier—not to show off his wit or his literature, but to support a party and bring about certain political action.

Now, in this last lecture, I should like to show him at work on a satire which he hoped would vex the world, and which was intended not merely to show off his wit or to reach a London or a Dublin audience, but which as he said later to the French translator of *Gulliver's Travels*, would be equally well understood abroad, and which was addressed both to his contemporaries and to posterity. If we were right in considering *A Tale of a Tub* as the final product of the seventeenth century, paradoxically growing out of it and at the same time satirizing it and repudiating so much of its spirit, so in like manner we may well regard *Gulliver's Travels* as, both in form and in shape, wholly the product of the eighteenth century, while being at the same time the most violent satire of its hopes and dreams and a repudiation of much that it most valued. For it is typical of the century in a very general way, because it is, more than all Swift's so-called historical writings, his contribution to the favourite study of the age—history, not of course in the present sense of the term, but as it was practised by the eighteenth century philosophers whether in France or in England, who were concerned, as Carl Becker has shown so conclusively in his *Heavenly City of the Eighteenth Century Philosophers*, all of them with a particular thesis on human behaviour, which they set out to prove, whether by a study of the Decline and Fall of the Roman Empire, or by the study of the history of England, or by a study of the spirit or ideas of Law.

They also like Swift used many of the weapons of the satirist—wit and ridicule and irony, even though their travels were limited to parts and places well-known. And Swift, like Gibbon, had learned his idea of liberty and justice from a study of the writers of Greece and Rome; he had given a good

80

deal of attention to the study of government, and by his own direct experience had arrived at as complete a scepticism as any of theirs. But these eighteenth century philosophers had "demolished the Heavenly City of St. Augustine only to rebuild it with more up-to-date materials"; they remained optimists enough to believe in the possible enlightenment and rescue of the human race from its folly and from its superstition. Swift had an answer very different from theirs, which has continued to shock successive generations, even though the course of later history has hardly proved him wrong. He thought of himself as different even from his friends, and he remained apart from and unlike most of the philosophers of the century. He could not share their beliefs, and he termed them "vous autres." Perhaps it was the purpose of Gulliver to prove this to them, and to their followers.

When his first political career was coming to an end, Swift like many other discarded statesmen turned to the writing of memoirs. He had wished to be appointed officially historiographer to the Queen, in order that he might leave a record for posterity. So after his return to Ireland in 1714, and indeed earlier in England after he left London, despairing of being of further use to the Ministry, he had immediately set to work to put down his own record of the history of the last four years of the Queen.

81

There are various manuscripts surviving from this period, one—*The Enquiry into the Behaviour of the Queen's last Ministry*—begun in the hand of Stella with corrections in the hand of Swift, but none of these memorials were printed in Swift's lifetime, and it was perhaps natural or inevitable that he should try to find some form in which he could make his comment on human behaviour for the benefit of his contemporaries as well as posterity. But this again could only be done safely and adequately in some disguise. For this purpose he could not appear as the London wit; a Bickerstaff would be too provincial and too literary, the Tory Examiner too political, the Dean too ecclesiastical, the linen draper of Dublin too Irish.

Once again he finds the solution by employing his favourite device of parody. He would write a book of Travels, in imitation of the most popular best sellers of the day, like Dampier's *Voyages*. It should not be forgotten also that in 1719, when Swift seems to have begun work seriously on *Gulliver's Travels*, that despised rival political pamphleteer, that secret henchman of Harley's, the fellow who was pilloried, whose name Swift could never remember, Daniel Defoe, delighted the world with his story of Robinson Crusoe. And so Swift settled down to read a lot of this trash, and turned over the pages of a seaman's manual in order to provide himself with the necessary flavour of nautical language, and emerged in an entirely new disguise, the one in which he is best known to the whole world—as the seaman, the plain honest traveller, not over learned or too literary (he had only been three years at Emmanuel College and after that had had some training as a surgeon and in navigation), a simple plain teachable man of unspoiled intelligence, who could serve as a sort of *Everyman.*

My Father had a small Estate in Nottinghamshire; I was the Third of five Sons. He sent me to Emanuel-College in Cambridge, at Fourteen Years old, where I resided three Years, and applied my self close to my Studies: But the Charge of maintaining me (although I had a very scanty Allowance) being too great for a narrow Fortune; I was bound Apprentice to Mr. James Bates, an eminent Surgeon in London, with whom I continued four Years; and my Father now and then sending me small Sums of Money, I laid them out in learning Navigation, and other Parts of the Mathematicks, useful to those who intend to travel, as I always believed it would be some time or other my Fortune to do. When I left Mr. Bates, I went down to my Father; where, by the Assistance of him and my Uncle John, and some other Relations, I got Forty Pounds, and a Promise of Thirty Pounds a Year to maintain me at Leyden: There I studied Physick two Years and seven

Months, knowing it would be useful in long
Voyages.

. . . I was Surgeon successively in two Ships, and
made several Voyages, for six Years, to the East
and West-Indies; by which I got some Addition
to my Fortune. My Hours of Leisure I spent in
reading the best Authors, ancient and modern;
being always provided with a good Number of
Books; and when I was ashore, in observing the
Manners and Dispositions of the People, as well
as learning their Language; wherein I had a great
Facility by the Strength of my Memory.

This device would also provide him with a way
to use all the hints and plans that had remained
from the evenings of the Brothers Club, or the satirical papers of Martin Scriblerus, or, even before
that, suggestions thrown out to Steele and Addison
for a Tatler: e.g., *Journal to Stella*, April 28, 1711:
"Yesterday the Spectator was made of a noble hint
I gave him long ago for his Tatlers, about an Indian
supposed to write his Travels into England. I repent
he ever had it. I intended to have written a book
on that subject." It is not fanciful to find here the
first source in Swift's mind of some of the comments
on English life of the King of Brobdingnag or of
the criticism of English morals made by Gulliver's
master in the land of the Houyhnhnms.

By employing the form of the travel book Swift
was able to use the satirical methods which he had

84

perfected in his earliest literary work, parody and raillery and irony, and to make use of all his experience of the world gained during his active political career, and make a masterpiece—the product of his mastery of his art together with his mastery of the business of life. It is this, I think, which gives such finality to his ethical judgments. It is sometimes said that Swift was not a great intelligence, that he was no profound scholar, no outstanding political thinker, and no really original genius. But at least that well-prepared, sceptical intelligence which showed itself in *A Tale of a Tub* had been given a rather complete and varied experience of the ways of the world and of the characters of men and women in those thirty years between his earliest writings and the appearance of *Gulliver's Travels*. He had met and known intimately the greatest and best men of his time, and he had likewise come up against and suffered from some of the cleverest and most ruthless scoundrels; he had had a price set on his head, and he had known what it was to be the idol of the mob, or, as he called them later, his good friends the common people of Ireland. He had indeed been himself a great traveller, and had learned many things; his problem was to find a way in which he could set down the most significant of his observations upon human life, so that the world might be forced to read them. For even if he could not do any good, he might be able to vex the world and perhaps amuse some of his friends.

In the first and the third books of *Gulliver's Travels* he manages to include a great deal of satirical reference to the political events in which he had taken part, both in England and in Ireland. Both of these books are in fact confused and inconsistent, because they are constantly twisted to suit his immediate satirical purpose, whether he is concerned with the political situation or with very specific parody and burlesque of the experiments of contemporary scientists or the schemes of other projectors.

There is a good deal of fun in Lilliput, and with Gulliver we are able to assume a certain superior detachment and amusement at the ways of the pigmies. Like him we are protected from any serious danger at the hands of the Lilliputians. We are provided as it were with a buff jerkin, which is proof against all their arrows; we are on good terms with them, and could not be unduly disturbed by anything those little creatures might do, who could dance, five or six of them at a time on the palm of one of our hands, or play at hide-and-seek in our hair. Even the diversions of the court of Lilliput are therefore inevitably observed by us with good humour, and we can laugh at the antics of the rope-dancers, and the *leaping* and *creeping* of the min-

isters as the Emperor advances or depresses his
stick. It is just a joke to watch them swearing an
oath according to the strange method prescribed
by their laws:

> hold the right foot in the left hand, place the
> middle finger of the right hand on the crown of
> the head, and the thumb on the tip of the right
> ear

—just another of the antics of these minute ballet-
dancers. And even the struggles between the High
Heels and the Low Heels, and between those who
break their Eggs at the Big End and at the Little
End, seem to be a matter for comedy; and that ugly
ambition of the Emperor to obtain all his enemy's
ships, after their Navy had been brought to him
by Gulliver, in order to make himself monarch of
the whole world, does not frighten us unduly, especially as his ambition is not approved by the wisest
part of his ministry.

We are indeed made very subtly to share the innocence of Gulliver, his unwillingness to believe
evil of princes, his unpreparedness for their ingrati-
tude and dishonesty. It was only after he had been
wrongly suspected of disaffection that he began
to have doubts:

> This was the first time [he says] I began to con-
> ceive some imperfect Idea of Courts and Ministers.

87

( We cannot really believe any harm of them, as the
Royal Family come to dine with him, sitting in their
chairs of state, with their guards about them, on a
corner of his table, just over against him; or as the
members of the Court visited him, remaining in
their coaches drawn by two horses gently round
his table. Even when the articles of impeachment
are drawn up against Gulliver, and the fierceness
of his enemies is disclosed, with their demand that
he should be horribly murdered, whereas the Emperor in his lenity and tenderness was willing to
condemn him only to the loss of his eyes, he is still
able to make use of the most delicate form of
irony: )

Yet, as to myself, I must confess, having never
been designed for a Courtier, either by my Birth
or Education, I was so ill a Judge of Things, that
I could not discover the *Lenity* and Favour of this
Sentence; but conceived it (perhaps erroneously)
rather to be rigorous than gentle. I sometimes
thought of standing my Tryal; for although I could
not deny the Facts alledged in the several Articles,
yet I hoped they would admit of some Extenua-
tions. But having in my life perused many State-
Tryals, which I ever observed to terminate as the
Judges thought fit to direct; I durst not rely on so
dangerous a Decision, in so critical a Juncture, and
against such powerful Enemies. Once I was strongly
bent upon Resistance: For while I had Liberty, the

whole Strength of that Empire could hardly subdue me, and I might easily with Stones pelt the Metropolis to Pieces; But I soon rejected that Project with Horror, by remembering the Oath I had made to the Emperor, the Favours I received from him, and the high Title of *Nardac* he conferred upon me. Neither had I so soon learned the Gratitude of Courtiers, to persuade myself that his Majesty's *present Severities acquitted me of all past Obligations.*

It is almost as though the very scale of the Lilliputians obliges him to handle them and their affairs with a sort of tenderness lest they break in pieces. The whole country remains inevitably in the imagination as a sort of toy-shop, invaded by a clumsy colossus who finds it difficult to move about without overturning houses and trampling on their inhabitants, unable even to see what is going on; amazed to observe "a cook pulling a Lark, which was not so large as a common fly; and a young girl threading an invisible needle with invisible silk." Only occasionally when Gulliver allows himself to make comments on the laws and customs of the land, and on their system of education, we sometimes forget the figure of Gulliver the colossus and the minute figures he is discussing, and hear rather the familiar comments of Dean Swift on education and life. It is surprising how easily the imagi-

89

nation is kept in leash if we are constantly given some one concrete detail, a goose the size of a sparrow, or a forest tree the top of which Gulliver can just reach with his closed fist; but likewise, a sentence or two can completely dispel the scene and banish us from this tiny commonwealth.

> In relating these and the following Laws, I would only be understood to mean the original Institutions, and not the most scandalous Corruptions into which these People are fallen by the degenerate Nature of Man.

Phrases like "the degenerate nature of man," "the great laws of nature," "the miseries of human life" are somewhat too large for that tiny world and break down the willing suspension of our unbelief; and then it takes more than the word *Lilliputian* to restore it again.

Swift was to find a better way of handling this problem of keeping in due balance the imagined scene and the real world in books II and IV, so that he could use quite freely every phase of his experience, and bring it to be weighed in the scales provided by his hosts.

But in the Third book, which as I have said is also somewhat confused and lacking in unity, his difficulty was not so much in forcing his satire to adapt itself to the imaginary circumstances of the voyage; it is rather that the material in part has never been thoroughly assimilated through his own experience, and he seems sometimes to fall back almost on the method of the *Tale* in making fun of the extravagancies of the virtuosos, and the strange experiments of the scientists of the Royal Society. A great deal has been written about the details of this book, to prove how closely he was parodying, when describing the experiments in the Academy of Lagado, the actual accounts he had read in the *Philosophical Transactions of the Royal Society*. In thus using his favourite method of parody which for full enjoyment requires an immediate recognition of the original, Swift was appealing more directly to his contemporaries and especially to his London audience, but he doubtless trusted that the absurdities he slightly exaggerated would serve as symbols which everyone could recognize of the spirit of research he was eager to expose. Professor Everett Case in his *Essays on Gulliver's Travels* published by the Princeton Press just before his recent death, is I think right in emphasizing that the satire upon Projectors in this book was not limited to virtuosos and scientists; for Swift was equally if not more concerned to warn his readers against the political projectors and speculators, who had been responsible for such schemes as the South Sea Bubble, and other trade swindles of this sort.

The real reason why so many readers have felt

that the Third book is confused and less effective than the others is not simply that Swift was making use of old stuff remaining from the days of the Scriblerus Club; it is rather that he was adding even after the rest of the book was finished passages of political satire in which he was tempted to celebrate his recent success in Ireland, a section indeed which seemed to the printer to be of so immediate and dangerous significance that it was not even included by Faulkner in his Dublin edition published ten years after the events referred to. And further Miss Marjorie Nicolson's and Miss Mohler's studies of the sources of the experiments in the Lagado Academy would indicate the likelihood that Swift, caught by the spirit of parody which he could never resist, went on even as late as the spring of 1726, when he spent some weeks in the company of Dr. Arbuthnot, collecting information about actual experiments then being carried out in order to burlesque them for his main purpose. Mr. Harold Williams in his introductory essay to my edition of *Gulliver's Travels* has drawn attention to Dr. Arbuthnot's letter of October 1725, in which he offers the latest information:

. . . before you put the finishing touch to it, it is really necessary to be acquainted with some new improvements of mankind that have appeared of late, and are daily appearing. Mankind has an inexhaustible source of invention in the way of folly and madness.

But he assumes that Swift did not avail himself of this offer, because a few days after the book was printed Arbuthnot commented:

I tell you freely, the part of the projectors is the least brilliant.

I myself am tempted to interpret that in the opposite way, for it must be remembered that they were two rivals in irony, and I cannot imagine that Arbuthnot would have been so indelicate as to have written just then almost in reproach, if Swift had indeed rebuffed his offers to help. But what more natural if he had provided Swift with material and advice for this section, than that he should say "Of course the part of the book which I interfered with is the least brilliant"?

In any case, the construction of parts of this book is less satisfactory. The materials used have not been properly matured, the wood is too green; and one would have to admit also that the position of the satirist himself is not a very secure one in some of his attacks upon the physical scientists, and the whirligig of time has given them their revenge.

But my argument is going to be that the real greatness of *Gulliver's Travels* is to be found when we recognize it as the final and completest satire

on human life of this Christian moralist. That is the
reason why so many people have been disturbed by
the book. Some have said: Do not listen to this fellow, because he is mad; or, He is a monster, uttering
blasphemies against mankind; or, He is abnormal,
incapable of ordinary affection and loyalties; do not
trust anything he says.

It is written by one who did not like the way
of the world and was not unwilling to set down his
testimony against it. Let me just remind you of two
passages which seemed to the original publisher so
unveiled, such unrestrained invective that he employed a clergyman, the Rev. Andrew Tooke, to
rewrite them in more cautious language; but Swift
was careful to have them restored in the edition he
prepared for his collected works. The first is a comment on English political life:

> The Bulk of the People consisted wholly of Dis-
> coverers, Witnesses, Informers, Accusers, Prose-
> cutors, Evidences, Swearers; together with their
> several subservient and subaltern Instruments; all
> under the Colours, the Conduct, and pay of Min-
> isters and their Deputies.

And then, with that curious delight in a sort of verbal game, he suggests a list of code terms, followed
by their mysterious meanings:

> For Instance, they can decypher a Close-stool to
> signify a Privy-Council; a Flock of Geese, a Sen-

94

ate; (a lame Dog, an Invader;) the Plague, a standing Army; a Buzard, a Minister; the Gout, a High Priest; a Gibbet, a Secretary of State; a Chamber pot, a Committee of Grandees; a Sieve, a Court Lady; a Broom, a Revolution; a Mouse-trap, an Employment; a bottomless Pit, the Treasury; a Sink, a C—t; a Cap and Bells, a Favourite; a broken Reed, a Court of Justice; an empty Tun, a General; a running Sore, the Administration.

The second is a comment on the legal profession, with which it must be admitted Swift had had some unfortunate experiences: and perhaps it should also be remembered that Gulliver had been living some time in the land of the Houyhnhnms, and had doubtless been influenced by their simple views, before making this explanation to his master:

I said there was a Society of Men among us, bred up from their Youth in the Art of proving by Words multiplied for the Purpose, that *White* is *Black*, and *Black* is *White*, according as they are paid. To this Society all the rest of the People are Slaves.

. . . Now, your Honour is to know, that these Judges are Persons appointed to decide all Controversies of Property, as well as for the Tryal of Criminals; and picked out from the most dextrous Lawyers who are grown old or lazy: And having been byassed all their lives against Truth and Equity, lie under such a fatal Necessity of favouring Fraud, Perjury and Oppression; that I have known some of them to have refused a large Bribe from the Side where Justice lay, rather than injure the *Faculty,* by doing any thing unbecoming their Nature or their Office.

. . . In the Tryal of Persons accused for Crimes against the State, the Method is much more short and commendable: The Judge first sends to sound the Disposition of those in Power; after which he can easily hang or save the Criminal, strictly preserving all the Forms of Law.

But there were other comments which occur in the second journey when Gulliver was trying to explain the glories of western civilization to the simple-hearted king of the Brobdingnagians, that the publisher did not bother to change, though the author's intention and the possible effect might be considered dangerous, for they were carefully covered in irony. Gulliver is still able to boast of the past history of his own people and to try to describe to the King some of the more important developments of society, becoming quite eloquent as anyone may easily do when abroad "to celebrate the Praise of our own dear country in a style equal to its merits and felicity." It took five audiences each of several hours, and then in a sixth his majesty, consulting his notes, proposed many doubts, queries and objections upon every article; and later he sums up his impressions in a fitting but unpleasant figure:

I cannot but conclude the Bulk of your Natives, to be the most pernicious Race of little odious Vermin that Nature ever suffered to crawl upon the Surface of the Earth. " 14

Great allowances of course have to be made for one living wholly secluded from the world, unacquainted with the manners and customs of other nations; and Gulliver adds another story to illustrate the effect of narrow principles and short views, resulting from a confined education:

I shall here insert a Passage which will hardly obtain Belief. In hopes to ingratiate my self farther into his Majesty's Favour, I told him of an Invention discovered between three and four hundred Years ago, to make a certain Powder; into an heap of which the smallest Spark of Fire falling, would kindle the whole in a Moment, although it were as big as a Mountain; and make it all fly up in the Air together, with a Noise and Agitation greater than Thunder. That, a proper Quantity of this Powder rammed into an hollow Tube of Brass or Iron, according to its Bigness, would drive a Ball of Iron or Lead with such Violence and Speed, as nothing was able to sustain its Force. That, the largest Balls thus discharged, would not only Destroy whole Ranks of an Army at once; but batter the strongest Walls to the Ground; sink down Ships with a thousand Men in each, to the Bottom of the Sea; and when linked together by a Chain, would cut through Masts and Rigging;

divide Hundreds of Bodies in the Middle, and lay all Waste before them. That we often put this Powder into large hollow Balls of Iron, and discharged them by an Engine into some City we were besieging; which would rip up the Pavement, tear the Houses to Pieces, burst and throw Splinters on every Side, dashing out the Brains of all who came near. That I knew the Ingredients very well, which were Cheap, and common; I understood the Manner of compounding them, and could direct his Workmen how to make those Tubes of a Size proportionable to all other Things in his Majesty's Kingdom; and the largest need not be above two hundred Foot long; twenty or thirty of which Tubes, charged with the proper Quantity of Powder and Balls, would batter down the Walls of the strongest Town in his Dominions in a few Hours; or destroy the whole Metropolis, if ever it should pretend to dispute his absolute Commands. This I humbly offered to his Majesty, as a small Tribute of Acknowledgment in return of so many Marks that I had received of his Royal Favour and Protection.

The King was struck with Horror at the Description I had given of those terrible Engines, and the Proposal I had made. He was amazed how so impotent and groveling an Insect as I (these were his Expressions) could entertain such inhuman Ideas, and in so familiar a Manner as to appear wholly unmoved at all the Scenes of Blood and Desolation, which I had painted as the common Effects of those destructive Machines; whereof he said, some evil Genius, Enemy to Mankind, must have been the first Contriver. As for himself, he protested, that although few Things delighted him so much as new Discoveries in Art or in Nature; yet he would rather lose half his Kingdom than be privy to such a Secret; which he commanded me, as I valued my Life, never to mention any more.

But it is after all the fable of the Fourth book which has most shocked Swift's readers, though it is a simple and traditional moral tale, rather vividly dramatized with the help of animal symbolism. It is perhaps a little mediaeval in its extravagant and sometimes unpleasant burlesque of some of the qualities of man's brute nature, and in the complete separation of his rational qualities as they might conceivably exist in some utopian world. But the real source of our fear of Swift's satire is that we are progressively led on with Gulliver from a comparatively happy condition in which we were in that blessed state of being well deceived—the serene peaceful state of being a fool among knaves—until we have made the painful discovery of the knavery of human life and of the stupidity and malice of mankind. But many moralists and prophets and satirists have made this same discovery and travelled by this same road, and have found the world a wilderness and life a sorry condition, and they have turned to the past or the future or to another world for consolation, and in some way or other have justified the fact of life/But Swift leaves us no escape, no place for dreams or imaginings; he can see no reason for it at all. He has not been able to keep out at any point in his travels this plain dislike of human existence, the protest of the individual against the sum of things,

a stranger and afraid.
In a world I never made.

But his protest is put in a quite simple non-romantic way, some development of the theme stated in one of his own Pensées, printed under the title, *Thoughts on Religion.*

Although reason were intended by providence to govern our passions, yet it seems that, in two points of the greatest moment to the being and continuance of the world, God hath intended our passions to prevail over reason. The first is, the propagation of our species, since no wise man ever married from the dictates of reason. The other is, the love of life, which, from the dictates of reason every man would despise, and wish it at an end, or that it never had a beginning.

This colours that passage in the sixth chapter of the Voyage to Lilliput concerning the relations between parents and children:

100

. . . they will never allow that a Child is under any
Obligation to his father for begetting him, or to his
mother for bringing him into the world; which
considering the miseries of human life, was neither
a benefit itself nor intended so by his parents,
whose thoughts in their love-encounters were
otherwise employed and therefore they conclude
that parents are the last of all others to be trusted
with the education of their own children.

More dramatically and more memorably he plays
with the same theme at the end of the Fourth book,
when, returning from his experience of a rational
Utopia under the influence of beings who were the
perfection of nature, Gulliver freely confesses that
the sight of his wife and family filled him "only
with Hatred, Disgust and Contempt; and the more,
by reflecting on the near Alliance [he] had to
them." This is further developed in the following
paragraph in a way which one cannot help feeling
afforded Swift the keenest satisfaction.

As soon as I entered the House, my Wife took
me in her Arms, and kissed me; at which, having
not been used to the Touch of that Odious Animal
for so many Years, I fell in a Swoon for almost an
Hour. At the Time I am writing, it is five years
since my last Return to *England:* During the first
Year I could not endure my Wife or Children in
my Presence, the very Smell of them was intoler-
able; much less could I suffer them to eat in the

101

same Room. To this Hour they dare not presume to touch my Bread, or drink out of the same Cup; neither was I ever able to let one of them take me by the Hand.

But even this is not such a violent satire upon "love of life" as Swift reserved for the last episode of the third voyage, which may well have been in point of composition the last chapter he wrote. For we know that he wrote the Fourth book mainly in 1723, and did not complete the Third—apart from final revisions—until 1725. It is a chapter entirely complete in itself—a perfect little irony. I cannot understand why it has not been more praised, and used in anthologies, or in books of piety. Swift himself draws particular attention to it, and evidently considered it to be quite original. He says:

I thought this account of the Struldbruggs might be some Entertainment to the Reader, because it seems to be a little out of the common Way; at least, I do not remember to have met the like in any Book of Travels that hath come to my Hands.

Gulliver is asked one day whether he had seen any of their immortals, and after hearing an account of them, indulges in his most endearingly innocent way in extravagant expressions of rapture at the thought of a people so blessed. He is then asked by his amused hosts what he would do if he were an immortal. After enlarging upon many topics "which the natural desire of endless life and sublunary happiness could easily furnish," he is told what the Struldbruggs are really like and finally has an opportunity to see five or six of them, the youngest not above two hundred years old.

> They were the most mortifying sight I ever beheld . . . and my keen appetite for perpetuity of life was much abated.

He would have been glad to send a couple home to arm people against the fear of death, but that was forbidden by the laws of the kingdom. Nevertheless, he tells us again with disarming innocence, he was led to believe that if he were to write down a simple and wholly truthful account of his travels, it might possibly do his countrymen some good. He can claim to be above any possible censure, having avoided every fault commonly charged against writers of travels:

> I write for the noblest End, to inform and instruct Mankind, over whom I may, without Breach of Modesty, pretend to some Superiority, from the Advantages I received by conversing so long among the most accomplished *Houyhnhnms*. I write without any View towards Profit or Praise.

Is Gulliver then after all only another moral tale, another rationalist's utopian dream to turn men from the folly of their ways and bring about some improvement in human society? Swift indeed allows Lemuel Gulliver to enter unsuspectingly the company of the eighteenth century philosophers, and to believe for a while, as even the most sceptical of them did, even a Hume or a Voltaire, that humanity could enter into a heavenly city of its own if only it could be released from the bonds of superstition and ignorance. But Swift allowed Gulliver to go thus far only to undeceive him utterly, and take from him his last illusion.

When the book appeared for the first time pretty much as Swift had written it, published under his direction in Dublin in 1735, it had been provided with an epilogue, in the form of a letter from Captain Gulliver to his cousin Richard Sympson, who had been responsible for getting the book printed. In this final statement Swift is careful to separate himself from the other historians and philosophers, and even from the rest of the satirists, turning his satire full upon them and their vain hopes to do something to improve the human species:

I do in the next place complain of my own great Want of Judgment, in being prevailed upon . . . very much against my own Opinion, to suffer my Travels to be published. Pray bring to your Mind how often I desired you to consider, when you insisted on the Motive of *publick Good;* that the Yahoos were a species of animal utterly incapable

of Amendment by Precepts or Examples: And so
it hath proved; for instead of seeing a full Stop
put to all Abuses and Corruptions, at least in this
little Island, as I had reason to expect: Behold,
after above six Months Warning, I cannot learn
that my Book hath produced one single effect according to my Intentions: . . . And, it must be
owned, that seven Months were a sufficient Time
to correct every Vice and Folly to which Yahoos
are subject; if their Natures had been capable of
the least Disposition to Virtue or Wisdom.

Swift could not escape from this final irony. He
did not wish to prescribe for the sickness of humanity, having no hope of its recovery; but he could
not refrain from probing, anatomizing and diagnos-
ing its malady, though convinced that the further
he went the more he would find to stir his indignation and his pity. And from his youth he had known
it and written it down with a kind of foolish pride,
that he was one

> whose lash just Heaven has long decreed
> Shall on a day make sin and folly bleed.

To the end it was his peculiar satisfaction as a moralist and a satirist, in all his various disguises, and
employing all the tricks of his trades, to make us
see what a world we live in, to make us feel its
brutality and its degradation, to disturb all our com-

placencies and to leave us unreconciled to the "un-estimable sum of human pain."

Although *Gulliver's Travels* is the one book by which Swift has been most widely and continuously known, it was not his last word as a moral satirist. For another twelve years he continued to write both in verse and in prose, stirred by the situation in Ireland, even when he had given up political satire as futile. For he could still give vent to his indignation, his bitterness and his scorn, even when he had no hope. He could continue to indulge in the luxury of satire, and find an escape from unprofitable political activity into pure irony.

He had 'been wearied out for many years with offering vain, idle, visionary Thoughts'; at length, 'utterly despairing of Success' he fell upon a Proposal 'wholly new,' of 'no Expense and little Trouble,' which he proceeds very quietly to set out in great detail as a means wholly unexceptionable *for preventing the Children of poor People from being a Burthen to their Parents or the Country, and for making them Beneficial to the Publick.* It is curious to note the similarity in tone, as he introduces us to his last irony, with the Apology, which he had written for *A Tale of a Tub*, twenty years before:

> He resolved to proceed in a manner, that should be altogether new, the World having been already

106

too long nauseated with endless Repetitions upon
every Subject.

But there is also an important difference. Then, he
promised his audience something altogether new,
out of consideration for them, because of the endless repetitions they had been obliged to listen to.
He was concerned with his audience, and with the
effect of his wit upon them. Now, the irony is re-
lated to his own weariness with endless repetitions
of projects and proposals, all impractical and stupid
because they bear, as he knows too well out of long
experience, no relation to the real state of affairs
in Ireland, and because they take no account of
the determined policy of the English government
to impoverish the Irish people. Then, like a show-
man, he was concerned to advertise an entirely
novel entertainment; now, wearied out and hope-
less, he nevertheless comes once more for the last
time to challenge in public those responsible for
the condition of the poor people in Ireland, by
proposing a scheme to which no one in England
or in Ireland could conceivably object. It meets all
difficulties and would give universal satisfaction.

It is a very simple plan, and he is able to work
out the economic and business details of the proposed new industry in a way which demonstrates
very clearly that it would be profitable to all con-

cerned. It would provide a new commodity for the
rich and a modest living for the poor. He calculates
that the children of the beggarly Irish can be reared
to the age of twelve months at a cost of about two
shillings to their parents, "rags included." Tolerably
nursed, they should weigh at that age about twenty-
eight pounds, and the carcass should make four
dishes of excellent nutritive meat, which would not
be dear at ten shillings. That would provide a reasonable profit, and further the plan would save the
country the maintenance of a hundred thousand
children, from two years and upward which would
increase the nation's stock fifty thousand pounds
annually. A further profit could be made out of the
skin, which, "artificially dressed, will make admir-
able gloves for ladies, and summer boots for fine
gentlemen."

It might seem at first sight that this *Modest Proposal* should be considered a political satire, for it
was carefully worked out for a particular situation
in Ireland at that moment; and it was ostensibly
an appeal to the people of Ireland to take certain
immediate action. But Swift is here parodying himself. The irony is partly in the parody; but the
weapon is in the hand of a moralist, not of a politician. The irony is also partly in the attitude adopted
by the writer. He has learned that he has no longer
any power as a politician; he is unable to influence

the government, though he had once been a highly successful government apologist; he is unable to rouse the people, though he had once been acclaimed by them as their leader and they had banded themselves together for his defence. He has only one satisfaction left—to carry the case before a higher court, to appeal to the conscience of mankind and bear witness before posterity, leaving them to answer his irony, and to decide in such a case—for there would be many others like it—what answer they would make to his modest proposal, what alternative they would have to suggest, which he had overlooked. Let the sentimentalists shudder, if only the oppressors of mankind might feel for a moment the sting of his irony, and the oppressed be stirred to madness; and justice and humanity be vindicated, even though they should be banished from the earth.